ATTENTION DEFICIT DISORDER

ABOUT THE BASIC PRINCIPLES INTO PRACTICE SERIES

This important series provides essential fundamentals of theory and technique across a broad range of topics. Designed as basic texts for both graduate and undergraduate courses, these contributions will also serve as solid introductions to new areas of investigation and related interest for the practicing psychotherapist.

BRUNNER/MAZEL
BASIC PRINCIPLES INTO PRACTICE SERIES
VOLUME 13

ATTENTION DEFICIT DISORDER

Diagnosis and Treatment from
Infancy to Adulthood

PATRICIA O. QUINN, M.D.

BRUNNER/MAZEL, *Publishers* • New York

Case histories in this book are either composites of several patients' histories or are stories submitted by actual patients or their families. Identities have been changed to protect patient confidentiality.

Library of Congress Cataloging-in-Publication Data

Quinn, Patricia O.
    Attention deficit disorder: diagnosis and treatment from infancy to adulthood / Patricia O. Quinn.
       p. cm.—(Brunner/Mazel basic principles into practice series; v. 13)
    Includes bibliographical references and index.
    ISBN 0-87630-811-6 (pbk.)
    1. Attention-deficit hyperactivity disorder. 2. Attention-deficit disorder in adults. I. Title. II. Series.
RJ506.H9Q548   1997
616.85'89—dc20   96-35535
                                                     CIP

Published by
BRUNNER/MAZEL, INC.
19 Union Square West
New York, New York 10003

Manufactured in the United States of America

10 9 8 7 6 5 4 3 2 1

CONTENTS

To Judith L. Rapoport, a friend, mentor,
and the person who 25 years ago set my feet on the
path of pursuing a career in the diagnosis and treatment
of individuals with ADHD. Thank you for the
privilege of knowing you and following
in your footsteps at least a
part of the way.

P.O.Q.

ACKNOWLEDGMENTS

There are many who supported me in this project, but I would especially like to thank the following individuals:

Kathleen Cortese, my assistant, without whose patience and persistence the bibliographies found herein would never have been completed.

Suzi Tucker and Natalie Gilman, my editors, for your understanding and kind words of encouragement.

Georgia DeGangi for your assistance in presenting the regulatory disordered infant in Chapter 2.

Thomas Walsh for reading the entire manuscript and offering your professional insights.

Patricia and Peter Latham for your expertise in making the law and ADD more clear and concise.

My husband and children for bearing with me when I was "working" all those nights and weekends, even on vacations.

And finally thanks to the many children and adults with ADD with whom I have had the privilege to work over a number of years. Knowing you has made it all worthwhile.

INTRODUCTION

What is ADD? Is ADD the cause of my problems? What can be done about it? Should anything be done? Will it go away? Questions, questions, questions!

Considerable attention has recently been directed to the problems associated with Attention Deficit Disorder (ADD)* in children, adolescents, and adults. You, as a clinician, are probably receiving an increasing number of inquiries about the diagnosis and the disorder. This phenomenon has occurred as a direct result of grass-roots efforts on the part of parent support groups and an increase in the general overall awareness by the public of the symptoms of the disorder; but ADD itself is not new.

As most of you are aware, one of the first discussions of the disorder was probably that by Dr. Still in the British medical journal *Lancet* in 1902. Even popular literature in the early 1900s reflected a knowledge of the symptoms of the disorder and its relationship to school performance. In his classic work, *The Rainbow*, published in 1915, D. H. Lawrence describes the character Tom Brangwen, a schoolboy, in the following passage. "He could not voluntarily control his attention. His mind had no fixed habits to go by, he had nothing to get hold of, nowhere to start from. For him there was nothing pal-

---

*The term ADD is used in this volume to include all aspects of the disorder and is at times interchangeable with the terms ADHD, AD/HD, or ADDH.

pable, nothing known to himself, that he could apply to learning. He did not know how to begin. Therefore he was helpless when it came to deliberate understanding or deliberate learning" (Lawrence, 1915/1991, p. 11).

Attitudes regarding the nature of the disorder are reflected in the various name changes that the syndrome has undergone over the years. When I wrote my first paper on the topic in 1970, I needed to do a great deal of my research on the subject in the cerebral palsy literature, as the name had only recently been changed from Minimal Brain Damage to Minimal Brain Dysfunction. Keeping the initials MBD granted some continuity and revealed that thinking about the disorder had changed from a "brain damage" model to that of a functional abnormality. Following this trend, Paul Wender, in his book *Minimal Brain Dysfunction in Children*, undertook in the early 1970s to hypothesize about the biochemical nature of the dysfunction.

The main symptom of hyperactivity as it manifests itself in school-aged children became the focus of much research in the 1970s, and the syndrome at that time became known primarily as the Hyperactivity Syndrome or Hyperkinetic Child Disorder. Only much later was it recognized that children could have attentional deficits without being hyperactive, prompting a name change in the American Psychiatric Association's *Diagnostic and Statistical Manual*, 3rd edition (*DSM-III*, 1980) to Attention Deficit Disorder (ADD) with and without hyperactivity. Adults were recognized as having the disorder, with the addition of a classification for Attention Deficit Disorder-Residual Type (ADD-RT).

The revised DSM-III (DSM-III-R, 1987) perhaps took a step backward with a labeling change to Attention Deficit Hyperactivity Disorder (ADHD). Subsequently, I spent many years explaining to patients and their parents that although all patients have this label, not all of them have the hyperactivity component. *DSM-III-R* also deleted the ADD-RT category, thus adding some confusion to the diagnosis of adults.

These problems were not completely rectified in the newest revision, *DSM-IV* (1994). The latest diagnostic criteria for ADD addressed the issue of adolescents and adults by the addition of wording in the diagnostic criteria for children. This revision also attempted to address the issue of ADD with and without hyperactivity by introducing criteria for two specific subtypes of ADD. These were designated ADD or ADHD, Predominantly Inattentive Type (A) (ADHD-I for short) or ADHD, Predominantly Hyperactive-Impulsive Type (B) (ADHD-HI for short). Individuals with symptoms in both of these areas could be coded as a third, Combined Type, (ADHD-C).

The basis for division into these two groups was provided by field trials conducted to determine how ADD appeared in children and adolescents (Lahey et al., 1994). The data from these trials suggested that, in nature, only two groups could be determined to exist based on factor analysis and cluster analysis. These data also suggested that hyperactivity and impulsivity were not two separate categories but that symptoms of hyperactivity were strongly associated with symptoms of impulsivity (McBurnett, 1995). Incidence figures reflected that 55% of children had ADHD-C, 27% had ADHD-I, and 18% had ADHD-HI (Lahey et al., 1994).

Through these field trials, it has become clearer that ADD symptomatology represents two distinct and probably different clinical entities. These new groupings also reflected the clinical consensus that ADD affects the three developmental areas of sustaining attention span, controlling impulses, and regulating activity level. Russell Barkley recently attempted to refine this theory by proposing that the inability to inhibit a behavior is the underlying problem for individuals with ADD. They simply act without thinking and cannot stop an action. They just go ahead and do whatever it is, regardless of the consequences. They do not plan ahead. Barkley summarizes, "It is this problem with behavioral inhibition that is the hallmark symptom of ADHD" (Barkley, 1994, p. 1).

Barkley further develops his concept of ADHD by utilizing

an already existing theory of Bronowski regarding human development. Bronowski speculates that our ability to inhibit and postpone a response to an event makes our thinking and language unique to our species. Barkley then goes ahead and applies this concept to ADHD (Barkley, 1994).

If an individual with ADD has a problem with inhibiting, Barkley speculates that, he or she should then also have problems with the four areas of mental abilities cited in Bronowski's theory, that is, prolonging an event in the mind, separating feelings from fact, self-directed speech, and breaking down and recombining events. After analyzing the behaviors of individuals with deficits in functioning in these four domains, Barkley ultimately concludes that the purpose of inhibiting before acting can be related to the primary executive functions of the brain (Barkley, 1994). Those cortical functions, as described by Denckla, include the ability to sustain attention, plan and sequence complex behaviors, inhibit inappropriate response tendencies, and sustain output over prolonged periods of time (Dencklla, 1989).

The conclusion that ADD is related to the executive functions of the brain receives validation from much of the scientific research conducted over the last two decades that has focused on brain structure as well as function and confirms the link between prefrontal and frontal cortex and disorders of executive function and ADD (see Chapter 1 for further discussion of this topic).

My experience in diagnosing and treating thousands of ADD children over almost 23 years of practice in developmental pediatrics has proven invaluable in establishing a practical knowledge base for dealing with this disorder. In addition, two of my own four children have been diagnosed with attention deficit disorder—one with ADHD and the other with ADD without hyperactivity. They have both also provided me with numerous opportunities for testing theoretical hypotheses and deciding on the value of various treatment modalities. In the following chapters, I hope to share with you the lessons learned and knowledge gained from both my practice and my own children.

ADD is a lifelong disorder. We now know that attentional deficits persist into adulthood and are pervasive across all domains of functioning, presenting problems to the individual, the family, and the community, either at school or in the workplace. The following chapters address ADD and the unique symptoms and problems exhibited at each developmental stage. In addition to the characteristic features of the disorder at a particular stage, criteria for diagnosis and treatment protocols are presented. Pertinent literature is reviewed and further readings on a particular subject are offered. Topics covered specifically address the unique needs of the individual during the period of development covered in that chapter. Diagnostic tools, such as behavioral checklists, questionnaires, and resource lists are included when appropriate. The resources provide additional materials of use to the clinician, teacher, and parents as well as to the child or adult who must deal with Attention Deficit Disorder and its aftermath.

As we begin this journey through the life span of ADD, let us first address the question "What is ADD?"

REFERENCES

American Psychiatric Association. (1980). *Diagnostic and statistical manual of mental disorders* (3rd ed.). Washington, DC: Author.

American Psychiatric Association. (1987). *Diagnostic and statistical manual of mental disorders* (3rd ed., rev.). Washington, DC: Author.

American Psychiatric Association. (1994). *Diagnostic and statistical manual of mental disorders* (4th ed.). Washington, DC: Author.

Barkley, R. (1994). More on the new theory of ADHD. *ADHD Report, 2,* 1–4.

Denckla, M. B. (1989). Executive functioning: The overlap zone between attention deficit disorder and learning disabilities. *International Pediatrics, 4,* 155–160.

Lahey, B. B., Applegate, B., McBurnett, K., et al. (1994). DSM-IV field trials for attention deficit/hyperactivity disorder in children and adolescents. *American Journal of Psychiatry, 151,* 1673–85.

Lawrence, D. H. (1991). *The Rainbow.* New York: Signet Classic Penguin Books. (Original work published 1915)

McBurnett, K. (1995). Attention-deficit hyperactivity disorder: Review of diagnostic issues for the DSM-IV committee. *DSM-IV Sourcebook.* Washington, DC: American Psychiatric Association.

Still, G. F. (1902). The coulstonian lectures on some abnormal physical conditions in children. *Lancet, 1,* 1008–1012, 1077–1082, 1163–1168.

Wender, P. (1971). *Minimal brain dysfunction in children.* New York: Wiley Interscience.

Chapter 1

WHAT IS ADD?

Attention Deficit Disorder (ADD) is a neurobiological condition that affects learning and behavior and is present in 3 to 10% of the school-age population (Wender, 1987). It begins in childhood and was initially thought to be outgrown by adolescence. However, we now know that this is not the case and that 30 to 70% of adolescents with ADD continue to be affected by symptoms into adulthood (Silver, 1992). But what is the evidence that this condition has a neurobiological basis?

THE NEUROBIOLOGICAL BASIS OF ADD

One of the first models used to explain ADD was the catecholamine hypothesis (Kornetsky, 1970). This theory refers to the faulty functioning in the brain of the neurotransmitters dopamine and norepinephrine. In 1977, Shawitz and coworkers determined that concentrations of the metabolite of dopamine in the cerebrospinal fluid in children with ADD was significantly lower than in a control group of normal children, suggesting reduced turnover of dopamine in this group. Another study (Rapoport, Quinn, & Lamprecht, 1974) found that plasma dopamine β-hydroxylase (DBH) activity was elevated in a group of boys with ADD who had high scores for minor physical anomalies. In addition, both imipramine and methylphenidate significantly increased plasma DBH activity. While the dopamine system was clearly implicated in this disorder, serotonin levels were not found to differ significantly in hyperactive children versus controls (Rapoport, Quinn, Scribanu, & Murphy, 1974).

Wender, in his book *Minimal Brain Dysfunction in Children*, published in 1971, was one of the first to propose that children with this disorder had an abnormality in the metabolism of the monoamines serotonin, dopamine, and norepinephrine. Although the role of serotonin in ADD has not been established on a biochemical basis, the newer serotonergic agents such as fenfluramine and fluoxetine have proven useful in treating comorbid conditions, such as depression, but they do not appear to address the core symptoms of inattention, impulsivity, and hyperactivity. While we can postulate that these monoamines are involved in ADD, biochemical studies have had only limited success in correlating measures of norepinephrine, dopamine, and their metabolites with the ADD syndrome (Zametkin & Rapoport, 1987). Nonetheless, a tripartite model of ADD involving dopamine, norepinephrine, and serotonin as causing the inattentive, hyperactive, and impulsive types of ADD respectively has recently been postulated by Voeller (1991).

IMPAIRMENTS IN BRAIN FUNCTIONING

Recent technological advances and refinements in neuro-psychological testing have led researchers to move beyond the catecholamine hypothesis in ADD and to look more seriously at anatomic structures in the brain and how impairments in their functioning could be related to symptoms of ADD. Further research has linked the frontal lobes, particularly the prefrontal cortex and limbic system, to motivation and emotional responsiveness. The executive functions, particularly attention and goal-oriented problem-solving behaviors, are also known to be dependent on the integrity of the frontal lobes and their subcortical connections, including the basal ganglia. Likewise, arousal states are modulated by interconnections with the reticular activating system within the deeper structures of the brain.

ADD has been described as a disorder of disinhibition and disregulation of the frontal cortex (Douglas, 1984; Gualtieri et al., 1985). In 1986, Chelune and coworkers also proposed a frontal lobe hypothesis for ADD. Neuropsychological studies were used to localize the disinhibition to the frontal lobes and resulted in the proposal that the symptom of hyperactivity was the direct result of a disturbed higher level of cortical inhibition. Since Chelune's work, other neuropsychological studies have confirmed frontal lobe disinhibition in individuals with ADD (Barkley et al., 1992).

More recently, neuroimaging techniques have allowed for further study of frontal lobe and striatal deactivation. Studies by Amen, Poldi, and Thisted (1993) reported significant prefrontal deactivation when individuals with ADD were asked to respond to an intellectual challenge. Some individuals in this study demonstrated decreased prefrontal activity even during rest. Lou and coworkers (1984) documented hypoperfusion in these same striatal areas of children with ADD, and Lubar and colleagues (1985) found abnormal brainwave activity in the frontal lobes of children with ADD when compared with controls.

Most exciting of all, however, were the landmark findings of Zametkin and colleagues at the National Institutes of Mental Health. In the *New England Journal of Medicine* (1990), these investigators reported convincing results from a study measuring glucose metabolism in the brains of adults who had histories of hyperactivity in childhood and who continued to be symptomatic. Each adult was the biological parent of a hyperactive child. Using positron emission tomography (PET) scanning techniques, this group measured regional cerebral glucose metabolism. Results indicated that this metabolism was lower in adults with ADD than in controls in both cortical and subcortical areas. Regions of greatest reduction were the premotor cortex and the superior prefrontal cortex. This study provided the documentation that these areas, which are responsible for control of attention and motor activity, were involved in the ADD syndrome.

Hynd and coworkers (1990), using magnetic resonance imaging (MRI) studies, have found differences in both the frontal areas and the corpus callosum of children with ADD. Results of an additional study in 1991 provided evidence of important differences in the morphology and size of certain areas of the corpus callosum in ADD children. More recent studies by Castellanos and colleagues at NIMH also indicate anatomic asymmetries on MRI scans of ADHD boys when compared to controls. Areas involved included the caudate, right frontal, globus pallidus and cerebellum (Castellanos et al., 1996).

AN INTEGRATED MODEL

These theories of frontal lobe disinhibition and the catecholamine hypothesis are not at odds but can be seen to complement each other. The prefrontal cortex has an abundant supply of catecholamines. In a review of the neurobiology of ADD by Zametkin and Rapoport (1987), dopamine was described as being localized in the limbic areas and assumed to be involved in the expression of ADD. Dopaminergic pathways are found between the motor cortex and the limbic center to the frontal areas. The prefrontal cortex also receives input from norepinephrine from lower brain structures. Thus the presence of both dopamine and norepinephrine in the prefrontal areas may be crucial to the functioning of the frontal lobes. Dysregulation of these systems impairs the capacity of the frontal lobes to perform properly. Consequently, both blood flow and metabolism appear to be depressed. Neuropsychological studies suggest that frontal areas are then unable to inhibit or control input from lower brain structures, resulting in the symptoms we see in ADD.

THE GENETICS OF ADD

Despite the varied clinical picture of ADD, investigators are now becoming more aware that ADD has a genetic basis. Studies of identical and fraternal twins (Gilles et al., 1992; Goodman & Stevenson, 1989) have found a significantly higher incidence of ADD in identical as compared with fraternal twins, suggesting a genetic predisposition. Other studies have discovered that relatives of ADD children are at greater risk for the disorder than are relatives of control children (Morrison and Stewart, 1971, 1973; Cantwell, 1972).

Research in molecular biology has also supported the concept of the heritability of ADD. Genetic studies of the dopamine D-2 receptor locus have found this to be a modifying gene in many neuropsychiatric disorders, including 46% of the patients with ADD. (Comings et al., 1991). Genetic transmission of ADD was also postulated, after research on a genetically inherited thyroid hormone disorder found that 70% of the children and 50% of the adults with generalized resistance to thyroid hormone also met the criteria for ADD (Hauser et al., 1993).

ADD IN GIRLS

Genetic factors clearly seem to be operating in the ADD syndrome, but the mode of transmission is not clear. Morrison and Stewart (1973, 1974) have proposed that polygenetic inheritance is the most likely mode of transmission for this condition. Gender differences do appear and ADD has always been reported to be more common in males than in females. Recently, however, girls have been diagnosed in increasing numbers as clinicians have become more aware of the disorder, particularly ADHD-I. In the latest DSM-IV field trials the ADHD-HI group contained 20% girls, with 27% diagnosed as ADHD-I and 12% found to be in the ADHD-C group (McBurnett, 1995). Recent predictions have even suggested that the male–female ratio may be as low as 3:1 or even 2:1, suggesting that hundreds of thousands of girls and women are affected by ADD.

Various factors may account for the phenomenon of missed diagnosis of ADD in females. Women with the disorder can escape even the best clinicians' detection, since they lack the typical symptoms of hyperactivity and impulsivity (Berry et al., 1985). In addition, girls tend to internalize more and develop the symptoms of anxiety and depression more often (Brown et al., 1989), thus presenting as patients with Mood Disorder as opposed to ADD. In their particular study Berry and coworkers found that girls with ADD further differed from males with ADD in that they demonstrated more cognitive impairments, particularly in the area of language function (Berry et al., 1985).

Differences were also seen in girls depending on whether the ADD was noted with or without hyperactivity. Girls with ADD without hyperactivity had poorer self-esteem and were usually older at the time of referral. All girls with ADD, regardless of whether they had hyperactivity or not, were reported to suffer more peer rejection; and research has shown that girls with ADD and hyperactivity tend to have more learning problems (O'Brien et al., 1994; Philips et al., 1993).

Girls with ADD may have increasingly severe problems beginning with the onset of puberty. These include increased emotional overreactivity, mood swings, and impulsivity thought to be due to an increase in hormones. Increased hormonal fluctuations throughout the phases of the menstrual cycle may also lead to more symptomatology (Hussey, 1990). In my practice I found that I was treating these girls with ADD for severe premenstrual symptoms (PMS) and mood swings with antidepressants as well as stimulants, long before the recent studies recommending the SSRIs to address these same symptoms were published.

Interest in these sex differences related to symptomatology and outcome led to a conference at the National Institutes of Mental Health in November, 1994. The purpose of the conference was to focus research attention on the presence of ADD in girls and women and to establish leading areas for future research. A summary of the recommendations and the data presented is yet to be published.

ADD WITHOUT HYPERACTIVITY

Recent research has now made clear that ADD without hyperactivity is a real entity and a valid diagnostic category. Lahey and Carlson's (1991) review of the literature on this topic established several points: First, factor analytic studies consistently indicate that covariation among the symptoms reflects two independent dimensions; second, ADD without hyperactivity exists as a clinical diagnosis; and third, children who meet the criteria for ADD *without* hyperactivity are behaviorally different from children who have the hyperactivity component. The latter children have far less serious conduct problems; they are less impulsive, less rejected by peers, and more withdrawn. They are also more likely to be characterized as sluggish and drowsy. An increased comorbidity including depression and symptoms of anxiety disorders was also noted in this group (Lahey & Carlson, 1991).

Significant differences between hyperactive and nonhyperactive children with ADD were also noted in both neurologic and cognitive areas. The overall percentage of prenatal and perinatal complications, neurologic abnormalities, impairments in visual perception, visual and auditory memory, reading, and writing were found to be significantly increased in those children with the hyperactivity. Whereas both groups were found to have abnormalities in these areas, the group of children with ADD-H had an increased frequency of these deficits, leading researchers to suggest that these children may have had an earlier brain insult resulting in impaired motor control as the cause of their abnormalities (Frank & Ben-Nun, 1988).

In children, for obvious reasons, the incidence of diagnosis of ADD without hyperactivity is clearly made less often than that of ADD with hyperactivity. Epstein and colleagues (1991) reported in their study that clinicians correctly diagnosed cases of ADD without hyperactivity only 50% of the time. In another study of 219 children, 5% were identified by teachers as having traits that satisfied the diagnosis of ADD without hyperactivity and 12% for ADD with hyperactivity (King & Young, 1982).

STABILITY OF THE DIAGNOSIS

As a consequence of these recent findings in genetics, anatomic functioning, brain-mapping research, and population studies, we have greatly expanded our knowledge concerning the etiology, genetic inheritance, and gender differences involved in having ADD. But what about the outcome and the natural history of the disorder?

ADD with hyperactivity has been reported to be one of the

most stable childhood diagnoses. In a study conducted by Cantwell and Baker (1989), 80% of children diagnosed with the disorder continued to carry the same diagnosis four years later. Rate of recovery was very low, only 9%, and approximately 15% of the children had comorbid conditions diagnosed at follow-up. These conditions included Depression, Overanxious Disorder, and Obsessive-Compulsive Disorder. However, the study showed a very different outcome for ADD without hyperactivity. The recovery rate was higher, at 20%, but comorbid conditions were still seen, including Depression and Conduct Disorder.

A 15-year longitudinal study of 369 children originally diagnosed in second grade and followed periodically until three years after graduation from high school also revealed continued difficulties. Children identified as having symptoms of ADD, later performed significantly more poorly in school and had poor social adjustment. Interviews in early adulthood continued to reveal differences in outcome for those earlier diagnosed with ADD (Howell, Huessy, & Hassuk, 1985).

Further information has come from retrospective studies of adults. One such study was a 25-year follow-up of adult males who, as children, had been diagnosed as having the "hyperactive child syndrome" (Borland & Heckman, 1976). In this study, 50% of the men continued to show a number of the symptoms of hyperactivity into adulthood, and nearly half had psychiatric problems. Despite normal intelligence and levels of education, these men had not achieved a socioeconomic status equal to that of their fathers or brothers.

In 1985, Paul Wender, observing that the symptoms of ADD both continued to exist and responded to treatment in adults, categorized such adults as having Attention Deficit Hyperactivity Disorder—Residual Type (ADHD-RT) (Wender 1981, 1985). Prospective studies that followed ADHD children into adulthood also found a persistence of the ADD symptoms. Underachievement and impulsivity with emotional liability were also seen. This group also expressed less satisfaction in areas of employment and marriage. Indeed only about half of the children diagnosed as having ADHD were functioning in the "normal" range at follow-up (Barkley, 1986).

Similar findings were reported in the follow-up studies reported by Weiss and Hechtman. In their sample, more than half of the hyperactive adults (66%) still had at least one disabling symptom of ADD. Restlessness was observed in 44% of the group and approximately one-fourth (23%) were diagnosed as having Antisocial Personality Disorder using DSM-III-R criteria. On several other measures, the hyperactive adults were also doing less well than controls (Weiss & Hechtman, 1993).

A more in-depth discussion of these and other results of outcome studies is provided in Chapter 7, Adults with ADD. However, it should be pointed out that in all the studies, half of the adults with ADD had a fairly good outcome. They were well adjusted and self-supporting, and although they might have one or two continuing symptoms related to this diagnosis, these were in no way significantly affecting their lives.

In order to further pursue investigation of the natural history of this disorder, each subsequent chapter of this book addresses a different period in the life cycle of the disorder. Each chapter presents the unique needs of the individual, methods of diagnosis, and briefly investigates therapeutic interventions particular to that stage of development.

REFERENCES

Amen, D. G., Poldi, J. H., & Thisted, R. A. (1993). *Evaluation of ADHD with brain SPECT imaging.* Paper presented at the annual meeting of the American Psychiatric Association, San Francisco, CA.

Barkley, R. A. (1986). Cited in G. Weiss & L. T. Hechtman. *Hyperactive children grown up.* New York: Guilford Press.

Barkley, R. A., Grodzinsky, G., & DuPaul, G. J. (1992). Frontal lobe functions in attention deficit disorder with and without hyperactivity: A review and research report. *Journal of Abnormal Child Psychology, 20,* 163–188.

Berry, C. A., Shaywitz, E. E., Shaywitz, B. A. (1985). Girls with attention deficit disorder—A silent minority: A report on behavioral and cognitive characteristics. *Pediatrics, 76,* 801–809.

Borland, B. L., & Heckman, H. K. (1976). Hyperactive boys and their brothers: A 25-year follow-up study. *Archives of General Psychiatry, 33,* 669–675.

Brown, R. T., Abramowitz, A. J., Madan-Swain, A., Eckstrand, D., & Dulcan, M. (1989, October). *ADHD gender differences in a clinical referred sample.* Paper presented at the annual meeting of the American Academy of Child and Adolescent Psychiatry, New York, NY.

Cantwell, D. P. (1972). Psychiatric illness in families of hyperactive children. *Archives of General Psychiatry, 27,* 414–417.

Cantwell, D. P., & Baker, L. (1989). Stability and natural history of *DSM-III* childhood diagnoses. *Journal of the American Academy of Child and Adolescent Psychiatry, 28,* 691–700.

Castellanos, F. X., Giedd, J. N., Marsh, W. L., et al. (1996). Quantitative brain magnetic resonance imaging in attention-deficit hyperactivity disorder. *Archives of General Psychiatry, 53,* 607–616.

Chelune, G. J., Ferguson, W., Koon, R., & Dickey, T. O. (1986). Frontal lobe disinhibition in attention deficit disorder. *Child Psychiatry and Human Development, 16,* 221–235.

Comings, E. E., Comings, B. G., & Muhleman, M. S. (1991). The dopamine D-2 receptor locus as a modifying gene in neuropsychiatric disorders. *Journal of American Medical Association, 266,* 1793–1800.

Douglas, V. I. (1984). The psychological processes implicated in ADD. In L. M. Bloomingdale (Ed.), *Attention deficit disorder: Diagnostic, cognitive, and therapeutic understanding.* New York: Spectrum Publications.

Epstein, M. A., Shaywitz, B. A., Shaywitz, J. L. & Woolston, J. L. (1991). Boundaries of attention deficit disorder. *Journal of Learning Disabilities, 24,* 78–86.

Frank, Y., & Ben-Nun, Y. (1988). Toward a clinical subgrouping of hyperactive and nonhyperactive attention deficit disorder: Results of a comprehensive neurological and neuropsychological assessment. *Journal of Diseases of Children, 142,* 153–155.

Gilles, J. J., Gilger, J. W., Pennington, B. F., & DeFries, J. C. (1992). Attention deficit disorder in reading-disabled twins: Evidence for a genetic etiology. *Journal of Abnormal Child Psychology, 20,* 303–315.

Goodman, R., & Stevenson, J. (1989). A twin study of hyperactivity, II: The etiological role of genes, family relationships and perinatal adversity. *Journal of Child Psychology and Psychiatry, 30,* 691–709.

Gualtieri, C. T., Ondrusek, M. G., & Finley, C. (1985). Attention deficit disorder in adults. *Clinical Neuropharmacology, 8,* 343–356.

Hauser, G., Zametkin, A. J., Martinez, P., et al. (1993). Attention deficit hyperactivity disorder in people with generalized resistance to thyroid hormone. *New England Journal of Medicine, 328,* 997–1001.

Howell, D., Huessy, H., & Hassuk, B. (1985). Fifteen-year follow-up of a behavioral history of attention deficit disorder. *Pediatrics, 76,* 185–190.

Hussey, H. R. (1990). The pharmacotherapy of personality disorder in women. Presented at the annual meeting of the American Psychiatric Association (symposia), New York, NY.

Hynd, G., Semund-Clikeman, M., Lorys, A. R., Novey, D., & Eliopulos, D. (1990). Brain morphology in developmental dyslexia and attention deficit disorder hyperactivity. *Archives of Neurology, 47,* 919–926.

Hynd, G., Semund-Clikeman, M., Lorys, A. R., Novey, E., Eliopulos, D., & Lyytinen, H. (1991). Corpus callosum morphology in attention deficit hyperactivity disorder: Morphometric analysis of MRI. *Journal of Learning Disabilities, 24,* 141–146.

King, C., & Young, R. D. (1982). Attentional deficits with and without hyperactivity: Teacher and peer perceptions. *Journal of Abnormal Child Psychology, 10,* 483–495.

Kornetsky, C. (1970). Psychoactive drugs in the immature organism. *Psychopharmocologia, 17,* 105–136.

Lahey, B. B., & Carlson, C. L. (1991). Validity of the diagnostic category of attention deficit disorder without hyperactivity: A review of the literature. *Journal of Learning Disabilities, 24,* 110–114.

Lou, H. C., Henriksen, L., Bruhn, P., Borner, H., & Nielsen, J. B. (1989). Striatal dysfunction in attention deficit hyperkinetic disorder. *Archives of Neurology, 46,* 48–52.

Lubar, J., Bianchine, K. I., Calhoun, H., Lambert, E., Brody, Z., & Nielsen, J. B. (1985). Spectral analysis of EEG differences between children with and without learning disabilities. *Journal of Learning Disabilities, 18,* 403–408.

McBurnett, K. (1995, Winter). The new subtype of ADHD: Predominantly hyperactive-impulsive. *Attention,* 10–15.

Morrison, J. R., & Stewart, M. A. (1971). Family study of the hyperactive child syndrome. *Biological Psychiatry, 3,* 189–195.

Morrison, J. R., & Stewart, M. A. (1973). Evidence for polygenetic inheritance in the hyperactive child syndrome. *American Journal of Psychiatry, 130,* 791–792.

Morrison, J. R., & Stewart, M. A. (1974). Bilateral inheritance as evidence for polygenicity in the hyperactive child syndrome. *Journal of Nervous and Mental Diseases, 158,* 226–228.

O'Brien, T., Phillips, W., & Stein, M. (1994). Gender differences in attention deficit hyperactivity disorder and attention deficit disorder—undifferentiated. Poster presented at the 5th Annual CH.A.D.D. Conference, San Diego, CA.

Philips, W., Gutermuth, L., O'Brien, T., Szumowski, E., & Stein, M. (1993). Gender differences in attention deficit hyperactivity disorder: Cognitive and behavioral characteristics. Poster presented at the American Psychological Society Conference, Chicago.

Rapoport, J., Quinn, P., & Lamprecht, F. (1974). Minor physical anomalies and plasma dopamine-beta-hydroxylase activity in hyperactive boys. *American Journal of Psychiatry, 131,* 386–390.

Rapoport, J., Quinn, P., Scribanu, N., & Murphy, D. L. (1974). Platelet serotonin of hyperactivity school-age boys. *British Journal of Psychiatry, 132,* 241–245.

Silver, L. (1992). Diagnosis of attention-deficit hyperactivity disorder in adult life. *Child and Adolescent Psychiatric Clinics of North America, 1,* 325–334.

Voeller, K. (1991). What can neurological models of attention, inattention, and arousal tell us about attention-deficit hyperactivity disorder? *Journal of Neuropsychiatry, 3,* 209–216.

Weiss, G., & Hechtman, L. T. (1993). *Hyperactive children grown up* (2nd ed.). New York: Guilford Press.

Wender, P. (1971). *Minimal brain dysfunction in children.* New York: Wiley Interscience.

Wender, P. H. (1987). *The hyperactive child, adolescent, and adult: Attention deficit disorder through the life span.* New York: Oxford University Press.

Wender, P. H., Reimherr, F. W., & Wood, D. R. (1981). Attention deficit disorders (minimal brain dysfunction) in adults. *Archives of General Psychiatry, 38,* 449–456.

Wender, P. H., Reimherr, F. W., Wood, D. R., & Ward, M. (1985). A controlled study of methylphenidate in the treatment of attention deficit disorder, residual type, in adults. *American Journal of Psychiatry, 142,* 547–552.

Zametkin, A. J., Nordahl, T. E., & Gross, M. (1990). Cerebral glucose metabolism in adults with hyperactivity of childhood onset. *New England Journal of Medicine, 323,* 1413–1415.

Zametkin, A., & Rapoport, J. (1987). The neurobiology of attention deficit disorder: Where have we come in 50 years? *Journal of the American Academy of Child and Adolescent Psychiatry, 26,* 676–686.

Chapter 2

ATYPICAL INFANTS AND TODDLERS

Children with ADD are a heterogeneous clinical population that has, over the years, received considerable attention in the pediatric and psychological literature. As many later behaviors may be seen as a continuum of the ongoing developmental process, several investigators have looked to the infant and toddler for clues to early diagnosis (Nichamin, 1972; Pasamanick et al., 1974; Schleifer et al., 1975). These atypical infants and toddlers are thought to be at risk for long-term difficulties, both academic and social. Early diagnosis and intervention may therefore be critical in affecting outcome (Wender, 1971; Werry, 1972; Rutter, 1982; Weiss &

Hechtman, 1986). In this chapter, factors considered to be influencial in the developmental process along with techniques for diagnosing the child at risk are explored.

Over the years in my clinical practice, I have followed many such "at risk" children. "Tiger" presents as a classic example of many factors relevant to the early diagnosis of attentional problems found in atypical infants that place them "at risk" for later difficulties.

> Tiger was born prematurely at 32 weeks gestation. Pregnancy was complicated by bleeding during the first trimester. Birth weight was 2300 grams. The neonatal course was uneventful except for some hyperbilirubinemia, which was treated with phototherapy. Tiger was breast-fed from birth. As an infant, he never slept for more than 10 to 20 minutes at a time and "catnapped" throughout the day and night. He never established a schedule or routine. Bath-time, instead of being a pleasant experience, was a nightmare. Tiger began to cry as soon as his clothes were removed and was screaming by the time he was placed in the water. Instead of being soothed by the water, he became rigid and was even bathed standing upright on occasion.
>
> At his early feedings, Tiger would gulp voraciously and then quickly give up and fall asleep. Later, when solid foods were introduced, Tiger refused many textures and spit out any "lumpy" foods. Mealtimes were literally a "mess" and soon became a struggle.
>
> The mother and father, as new parents, were quickly frustrated but his mother, especially, felt that she was inadequate and a failure at "mothering" her child. These parents sought help from their pediatrician, but the standard responses such as "Let him cry himself to sleep" or "He'll outgrow it" never seemed to apply to Tiger. In desperation, his parents contacted their local hospital's intensive care nursery developmental follow-

up clinic and were referred to an occupational therapist and social worker. Counseling helped the parents
to understand the problems Tiger faced and assisted
them in sorting out their feelings. Massage and various stimulation techniques helped soothe Tiger. Soon
they were able to establish a routine and Tiger became
considerably less irritable.

Tiger, however, remained "stubborn," and oppositional behaviors surfaced early in the second year. While
motor milestones appeared appropriately, Tiger's language skills lagged behind those of his peers. By age 3,
Tiger was considered "hyperactive" by both his parents and preschool teachers and a developmental evaluation was undertaken.

As many of the children with attentional and learning difficulties manifest problems from early childhood, it is important to ascertain which factors in the child's developmental or
family history may prove useful to the clinician in predicting
later deficits.

OBSTETRIC COMPLICATIONS

As early as 1956, Pasamanick and colleagues reported a higher
incidence of pregnancy complications for children with behavior disorders when compared with controls (Pasamanick et al., 1956). Several other studies have confirmed
this hypothesis in groups of children with ADD (Smith, 1972;
Minde et al., 1968; Wolff, 1967; Knoblock & Pasamanick,
1962) while others (Werner et al., 1968) have not been quite
as conclusive.

Nichols (1980), examining the findings of the Collaborative Perinatal Project, which followed children from 60,000
pregnancies until they were 7 years old, reported several factors that were associated with later hyperactivity. These in-

cluded maternal smoking during pregnancy, obstetric and birth complications, presence of hyperactivity in a sibling, and father's absence from the home.

PREMATURITY AND LOW BIRTH WEIGHT

ADD has for years been linked to the outcome of both premature and small-for-date (low birth weight for length of gestation) infants (Lubchenco et al., 1975; Fitzharding & Steven, 1972). Follow-up studies of infants born prematurely or with very low birth weights (McCormick et al., 1990, Hoy et al., 1988) have revealed higher levels of behavior problems, especially those characterized by hyperactivity, at school age in those children with very low birth weights (LBW). All LBW infants appear to have the same risk for developing behavior problems, as later reported by their mothers, when compared with normal-weight infants. A subsequent follow-up study found that 29% of infants in this LBW group had behavior problems and concluded that children with very low birth weights had higher rates of adverse health status at early school age across several dimensions of health, including behavioral disturbances (McCormick et al., 1992).

Further follow-up, examining classroom behavior in this group during elementary school (mean age 9.16 years), revealed that all low birth weight children (LBW) had lower attention and language skills, poorer scholastic competence, and higher daydreaming and hyperactivity scores than normal-birth weight children.

Girls were found to have fewer behavior problems than boys. The classroom behavior of LBW children was rated by teachers as poor, even for children who had not failed a grade, leading researchers to conclude that even LBW children who are on grade level still may be at risk for school problems (Klebanov, Brooks-Gunn, & McCormick, 1994).

Likewise, in a 1990 study evaluating social competence and

behavior problems in infants weighing less than 1500 grams, Ross and coworkers found that both premature boys and girls had significantly lower social competence scores on the Child Behavior Checklist when these children were 7 to 8 years old. Premature boys were found to have higher behavior problem scores, particularly on behaviors associated with conduct disorders. Researchers further reported that there appeared to be an interaction between prematurity and social class on the Behavior Problem score with the greater discrepancy seen in the lower-class group (Ross, Lipper, & Auld, 1990).

MINOR PHYSICAL ANOMALIES

Another series of studies (Quinn & Rapoport, 1974; Rosenberg & Weller, 1973; Steg & Rapoport, 1975; Waldrop & Halverson, 1971) found an association between frequency of minor physical anomalies (MPAs) of hands, feet, head, ears, face, and mouth and behavior problems in early childhood. These anomalies are thought to be the result of a disruption in the formation of these features in the first trimester of fetal development, and a genotype-phenocopy model was proposed to account for the varied factors that control this process (Rapoport & Quinn, 1975). It was noted that children with many MPAs and hyperactivity were more likely to have had an early onset of hyperactivity (before the age of 3) as well as either a maternal history of obstetric difficulties or a paternal history of hyperactivity (Quinn & Rapoport, 1974).

MPAs are detectable at birth and stable during early and middle childhood (Waldrop & Halverson, 1971). Their measurement in the infant has been proposed to be useful either alone or in combination of other variables to identify infants at risk for behavioral problems in early childhood. Waldrop et al. (1978) did indeed find a predictive effect for problems observed within a sample of 30 males attending preschool who were screened at birth. Quinn and Rapoport (1977) also conducted a screening of 933 normal newborns. Follow-up of these infants indicated that a higher number of anomalies was significantly associated with difficult behaviors at ages 1 and 2 for both males and females. At 1 year there was a positive relationship between high MPA scores and irritability and a positive family history of learning and/or behavior problems and obstetric complications. Reported allergies at both 1 and 2 years were also found to be associated with hyperactive or difficult behaviors.

NEUROLOGIC ABNORMALITIES

Denhoff and coworkers (1972), analyzing the data from the Brown University component of the Collaborative Perinatal Project, found that major and minor neurologic signs observed at birth and in the first year of life were associated with inefficient learning skills and poor school performance at 7 years. Infants were rated at birth and again at 1 year. Examination focused on muscle tone and movement and rated subtle differences found in several areas.

Scored ratings of multiple outcome items, including these abnormal neurologic findings, were found to be better at identifying those "psychoneurologically inefficient" children at age 7 than isolated measures such as prematurity or Apgar scores. Cases that emerged as being recognized early included infants in the "hyporeactive" and "hyperreactive" categories. These included signs such as lethargy, abnormal cry, jitteriness or tremulousness, and hyperactive behavior, the latter being most frequently found (Denhoff et al., 1972).

INFANT TEMPERAMENT

After the initial work of Rutter and associates in the area of temperament and behavior, researchers began to investigate infant temperament as a predictor of later behavior problems. These studies determined that quantitative measurement of children's behavioral styles, even as early as 12 to 24 months, could predict to a significant extent those children later referred to a psychiatrist; that temperamental difficulties antedated the onset of behavioral symptoms; and that specific patterns of functioning could be determined (Rutter, et al., 1964; Thomas, Chess, & Birch, 1968; Thomas & Chess, 1977).

In 1970, Carey devised a temperament questionnaire based on the work of Chess and Thomas, which he expanded in 1972 (Carey, 1970, 1972a). Temperament was measured for nine categories and was described by Carey as "the emotional reactivity or behavioral style displayed in the early months of life.... It refers neither to the individual's internal psychological organization nor to his abilities or other content of his behavior" (Carey, 1972b, p. 823). Infants with difficult temperaments are reported to have a high frequency of other problems, such as colic, sleep disturbances, night waking, (Carey, 1974) and irritability. They are less interactive and cuddly. In his early studies, Carey found an association with the incidence of colic, development at 1 year, and the frequency of injuries (Carey, 1972b). Difficult temperament in infancy was also found to be associated with poor school adjustment (Carey et al., 1977). This scale was revised in 1978 (Carey & McDevitt, 1978).

These temperamentally difficult infants were found to have behavior problems by the age of 2 or 3 years in other studies as well (Earls, 1981). Three temperamental characteristics, specifically, were related to poor behavioral adjustment at 3 years. These included low distractibility, high intensity, and high adaptability. High activity ratings in infancy were also found to relate to negative mood in girls at 3 years of age. Low distractibility appeared to be the single most important predictor of later behavioral adjustment. However, in this study, the term "low distractibility" does not refer to attention span and concentration, as one usually thinks of the use of this term. Rather, it refers to items that compose this category, including stubborn, resistant, or oppositional behaviors. An infant exhibiting this behavior would be stubborn and could not easily be distracted from following his or her own agenda, thus having a "low distractibility" score (Earls, 1981).

In a later study of infant temperament and school-age behavior, Wasserman and colleagues (1990) reported that initial analysis revealed that low socioeconomic status, ratings of difficult temperament, and perceptions of temperamental difficulties at 4 months were associated with increased maternal ratings of behavior problems at age 6 years. Teacher behavior problems scores were found to be positively associated with only low socioeconomic status. Their results suggested that the "link between difficult infant temperament and later behavior problems is complex and probably reflects both a child factor and parent attitudes about what constitutes typical infant behavior" (Wasserman et al., 1990, p. 801).

STABILITY OF RATINGS OVER TIME

In discussing the value of looking at possible infant predictors of later behavior problems, particularly as precursors of hyperactivity, it is important to address the issue of whether these findings have proved stable over time.

This issue has been investigated in several studies. The Fels Research Institute Study (Kagan & Moss, 1962) examined a nonclinical sample with respect to motor activity and determined hyperactivity ratings to be stable over time. In addition, the Berkeley Growth Study (Schaefer & Bayley, 1963) following infants from birth to 36 months with a variety of behavioral measures found that only the early infancy rating of activity predicted similar behavior in later childhood.

The New York Longitudinal Study (Rutter et al., 1964) concluded that behavior ratings in the first 6 months and at 1 year did not have any predictive characteristics during the school years, but that significant differences were noted for behavior reported at 2 years. This seemed to be the point in time when temperament became associated with the development of other behavior disorders as well. This finding coincides with other reports indicating that behaviors at 2 or 3 years are more predictive of later disabilities than earlier ratings.

This complex question regarding infant predictors was again more recently addressed by a group of researchers from Australia (Oberklaid et al., 1993) who studied a large community sample of 1,583 to determine whether preschool behavior problems at age 4 and 5 years could be predicted from infant temperament and other values in infancy. From this study it was concluded that the best predictor of later problems was the combination of mothers' overall ratings of temperament and their report of infant behavior problems, especially when combined with other infant variables such as perinatal stress, male sex, and a non-Australian parent.

However, of even greater significance was the finding that it was the mother's perception that a child was difficult that was most important. This perception combined with other variables was a far more powerful predictor of preschool behavior problems than the ratings of difficult temperament themselves, thus confirming the need to listen to the complaints and concerns of the mother and take these concerns seriously!

DEVELOPMENT OF ATTENTION
SPAN IN INFANTS

But when and how does attention span develop in infancy? How can it be measured?

Michael Lewis has presented voluminous data on the development of attention and perception in the infant and young child as a measure of early cognitive growth (Lewis, 1971). Lewis's findings were based on the concept that response decrement (losing interest) and recovery to visual and auditory stimuli over time was a function of age, with older infants showing the greatest decrement and response recovery. Significant relationships were found between response decrement and faster learning as well as a correlation with full-scale Stanford-Binet IQ scores at age 4 years. Lewis's comparison of normal infants and infants with central nervous system dysfunction consistently revealed significantly slower response decrements for the pathological groups. He therefore concluded that "the degree of response decrement can be used as an important indicator of CNS dysfunction as well as of cognitive development and learning" in infants and young children (Lewis, 1975, p. 153).

This concept was supported by a study published in 1981 by Schexnider and coworkers, which looked at visual habituation in a group of 12-month-old male infants who were identified as being "at risk" of developing later attentional problems on the basis of a high minor physical anamoly (MPA) score at birth. Slower response decrement was observed in the high-MPA infants tested in a low task-demand condition and was consistent with Lewis's findings in infants with various forms of brain pathology (Schexnider et al., 1981).

Jerome Kagan (1970) also analyzed the determinants of attention in the infant and delineated three factors that were felt to influence attention change during the first 2 years. He reported that a high rate of change in physical aspects of the stimulus was primary during the initial weeks and that small infants can pay attention for only a brief period unless the stimulus is changed frequently. Fast-moving or light-dark contrasting colored objects will cause changes rapidly, thus holding a newborn infant's attention.

By 2 months, discrepancy was seen as the major factor in determining attention. This ability was dependent on the formation of a schema for certain objects. It was the discrepancy from such a schema that then held the infant's attention. Thus, after the infant has formed a schema of the human face, a face moderately discrepant from the schema of a face will hold its attention longer. However, if the face is extremely discrepant at this point, attention or fixation is reduced.

Kagan (1970) further proposed that "activation of hypothesis" became influential at around 12 months. This related to the interpretation of the meaning of a stimulus and allowed a young child to interpret the meaning of speech sounds as language. For example, the child will listen and realize that a certain combination and intonation may mean that it is bath time. The more extensive the repertoire of hypothesis and the more knowledge the child has, the longer he can work at interpretation and the more prolonged the child's attention (Kagan, 1970).

It was felt that these three factors supplement each other in the older infant and toddler. Kagan postulated that the influence of these three factors was probably not limited to the first 2 years of life and that "the central problem in educating children is to attract and maintain focused attention" (Kagan, 1970, p. 305).

Following these same lines of investigation, clinicians at the Reginald Lourie Center in Rockville, Maryland, have recently introduced a specific test designed to provide an overall measure of sustained attention in infants ages 7 to 30 months. This *Test of Attention in Infants* (TAI) (DeGangi, 1995) is capable of differentiating infants with normal attentional abilities from those with attentional deficits; it provides important diagnostic information that can be useful in educational and therapeutic programming as well as diagnosis. The TAI is specifically targeted for the infant and toddler who may be "at risk" for later cognitive delays, attentional deficits, and learning disabilities and provides important diagnostic information that can be used in educational and therapeutic programming (DeGangi, 1995).

There are five age-specific versions of the TAI. Eight common activities are presented for each of the age ranges, providing an overall measure of sustained attention. The test focuses on the components of attention that have been found to be useful for information processing. These four main areas of attention include the ability to initiate and sustain attention during novel events; persist and maintain interest in a given task over time; self-initiate organized adaptive motor, visual, or social responses while sustaining attention; and shift attention between stimuli and focus attention when competing stimuli are present (DeGangi, 1995).

REGULATORY DISORDERED INFANTS

In addition to focusing on attention, recent research has begun to reinvestigate the clinical importance of "fussy" or difficult behaviors in infants, independent of difficult temperament. The developmental histories of preschool and school-aged children with learning and/or behavioral problems often includes both the symptoms of a difficult temperament *and* sensorimotor deficits. Greenspan (1981) described the behaviors of these dually affected infants and postulated that they were at risk for psychopathology and later learning difficulties.

DeGangi (1991) further expanded Greenspan's initial work and recognized these infants as being regulatory disordered. These infants were felt to be hypersensitive to auditory, tactile, visual, and vestibular stimuli (DeGangi & Greenspan, 1988). Symptoms manifested include fussiness, irritability, poor self-calming, intolerance for change, and a hyperalert state of arousal (DeGangi, 1993; DeGangi, DiPietro, Greenspan, & Porges, 1991). Regulatory disordered infants have difficulty with sleep, self-consoling, feeding, arousal, mood regulation, and transitions. The percentage of infants having problems in these various domains is contained in Table 1. It should be noted that the prevalence of problems in any one category was less than 3% for a normal sample.

TABLE 1
Regulatory Disordered Sample

Domain	Age Range (in months)				
	7–9	10–12	13–18	19–24	25–30
Self-regulation	89%	89%	92%	92%	64%
Attention	0%	0%	23%	31%	43%
Sleep	39%	57%	38%	15%	21%
Feeding	0%	28%	0%	38%	0%
Tactile	50%	71%	83%	85%	57%
Movement	17%	14%	42%	54%	36%
Listening	0%	43%	50%	62%	0%
Visual	11%	43%	42%	23%	21%
Emotional	28%	71%	83%	38%	14%
Mean percent of behaviors listed above	26%	46%	50%	49%	28%

Source: "Infants at-risk: The symptomatology of regulatory disordered infants," by G. DeGangi, 1993, Developmental Dialogue, Vol. 4, No. 1. Copyright © 1993 by Reginald S. Lourie Center for Infants and Young Children. Reprinted with permission.

Hyperactivity and inability to organize attentional responses may also be present in these regulatory disordered infants. Preliminary studies of these infants with follow-up to 4 years indicates that they are at high risk for perceptual, language, sensory integrative, and behavioral problems in the preschool years. A high incidence of sensory integrative deficits, tactile defensiveness, motor planning problems, hyperactivity, and emotional and behavioral problems were present in the regulatory disordered population at 4 years of age, suggesting that untreated regulatory disordered infants may not outgrow behavioral difficulties (DeGangi et al., 1993).

DIAGNOSIS OF INFANTS AND TODDLERS

In order to establish appropriate intervention strategies to assist the "at risk" infant and young child, in the clinical setting it is of foremost importance to determine how these atypical infants will present to you as a clinician. What are some of the clues to early diagnosis? What have we learned from the preceeding information and scientific studies?

Characteristic Symptoms and Physical Findings

A common early presentation of infants at risk for later developmental deviations involves the reporting of self-regulatory problems beyond the initial 6-month period, when these issues usually resolve in most infants. These problems include frequent reports of difficulty with arousal, deviant attentiveness, crying, irritability, and sleep disorders. Sleep disorders may be a prominent feature and the infant may never achieve the ability to sleep through the night, with frequent wakings occuring each night. Naps are abandoned early, and the young toddler may be described as requiring little sleep.

Parent-child interactions are affected by infant temperament, and the parent later perceives that the toddler has both a difficult temperament and problem behaviors. The need for effective parenting and coping skills is heightened. Parents who were able to parent a previous child satisfactorily now find that they are at a loss in dealing with this particular infant or toddler.

Neurologic dysfunction seen on examination during the first year may be an early indicator of later neurodevelopmental deviations in learning and/or attention. These infants may be seen as either "hyporeactive" or "hyperreactive." Hyporeactive findings include hypotonia, hypoactivity, and lethargy. Hyperreactivity is characterized by abnormal or asymmetrical primitive reflexes, abnormal cry, hypertonia, jitteriness, and hyperactivity in the young infant.

MPAs may be observed on careful examination. These include minor variations during development of the head, hands, feet, ears, face, and mouth. Scoring is done using the modified Waldrop method (Waldrop, Pedersen, & Bell, 1968). Mean anomaly scores are usually around 3.5. Zero to 3 is therefore considered a low anomaly score, while a score above 5 is considered a high anomaly score (Quinn & Rapoport, 1974).

While developmental milestones are usually appropriate, some infants may have delays in motor areas. Dyskinesias or abnormalities with motor movements may also be seen. Abnormal responses to sensory stimuli and deviant attentiveness may be present.

Overaggressive and oppositional behavior styles occur in some toddlers. Low frustration tolerance leads to an increase in temper tantrums, and infant's and young toddler's have great difficulty being consoled. Problems with transitions and sensitivities to tactile stimulation make daily routines such as bathing, dressing, and diaper changing difficult.

Hyperactivity and short attention span are observed. These children are always on the go, and some parents when questioned about the age at which the child first walked, will report that the child never walked but that he "ran" from the very beginning. Accident-proneness occurs, and studies have reported an increased number of surgical repairs in these young children.

CHECKLISTS AND QUESTIONNAIRES

Carey's *Revised Infant Temperament Questionnaire* for identifying problems in infants may be used in pediatric practices to rate infants in nine categories. These include activity, rhythmicity, approach, adaptability, intensity, mood, persistence, distractibility, and threshold. With the use of these ratings, the infant can then be categorized as falling in one of five clinical diagnostic groups: difficult, slow to warm up, intermediate high (difficult), intermediate low (easy), and easy. The frequency of occurrence within these categories for infants with behavioral disturbances is as follows: difficult (9.4%), slow to warm up (5.9%), and intermediate high (11.3%) (Carey & McDevitt, 1978). This revised questionnaire has good test-retest reliability and correlates well with mothers' general impressions.

The Toddler Temperament Scale was developed specifically for the 1- to 3-year-old group and has been utilized in numerous studies (Fullard, McDevitt, & Carey, 1984). It is based on the New York Longitudinal Study conceptualization of temperament with nine underlying dimensions. It is a 97-item scale on which parents are asked to rate the child's current behavior in a defined daily situation. Each item is rated on a 6-point scale from "almost never" to almost always."

As a result of the studies carried out at the Reginald Lourie Center, a symptom checklist has been designed for use by clinicians to assist in the identification of sensory and regulatory disordered infants from 7 to 30 months of age. The *Infant/Toddler Symptom Checklist: A Screening Tool for Parents* (DeGangi et al., 1994), designed as a parent report measure, focuses on the infant's response in the following domains: self-regulation, attention, sleep, feeding, touch (including dressing and bathing), movement, listening (including language and sound), looking and sight, and attachment/emotional functioning. The checklist itself has six versions: a single short version for general screening purposes and five age-specific screens. It is seen as a useful tool for screening infants to document the early signs of sensory integrative disorders, attentional deficits, and behavioral or emotional problems, thus initiating the referral of these at-risk children for more extensive evaluation and intervention.

Diagnostic Classification System for Infants and Toddlers

Clinicians may also be interested in using or familiarizing themselves with the *Diagnostic Classification of Mental Health and Developmental Disorders of Infancy and Early Childhood,* edited by Stanley Greenspan and Serena Weider (1994). (See "Resources for Professionals" on pp. 33–34 for further information.) This manual provides a framework for diagnosing emotional and developmental problems in children 3 years of age and younger. It addresses disorders missing from other classification systems and provides a description of the earliest manifestation of problems commonly diagnosed in older children and adults.

TREATMENT OF INFANTS WITH ATTENTIONAL DEFICITS

Intervention Programs

It is hoped that through the early identification and detection of those infants with attentional deficits and disordered regulatory systems it may be possible to initiate intervention programs that deal with both neurologically based behaviors and subsequent parent–infant interactions to prevent the development of more serious problems.

DeGangi and coworkers have addressed the issue of an intervention program and have proposed that "A comprehensive and integrated model of assessment and treatment is needed to address the constitutional problems of the regulatory disordered child and the impact of these problems on the family and the parent–child dyad" (DeGangi, Craft, & Castellan, 1991, p. 10). Thus, their treatment model includes parent guidance that focuses on management, child centered activities, and the use of sensory integration techniques that normalize sensory responses. This model clearly recognizes the stress that coping with a difficult child places on the family and a marriage and provides the support services that address the problems not only of the infant but of his parents and caregivers as well.

Support groups, parenting education classes, as well as individual and family therapy have all proven useful in helping parents deal with their child and their feelings. Home visitation may be necessary to address behavioral issues at the source. Structured behavior management programs work quite well with toddlers, but the concepts for carrying out such a program properly will have to be introduced to the parents. In addition, parents will need support from the professionals in order to keep the program going and deal with subsequent issues as they arise.

CONCLUSION

By assessing infants and toddlers and diagnosing attentional and self-regulatory problems early, it is hoped that mental health professionals, early childhood special educators, and occupational and physical therapists can intervene to address the neurologic deficits, disorganization, and poor self-monitoring that affect these children and contribute to their later disabilities. It is the role of the clinician to identify these children as early as possible and thereby make a difference with prompt referral to the appropriate professional or program.

RESOURCES FOR PARENTS AND CAREGIVERS

A Parent's Guide to Understanding Sensory Integration, 1991, Torrence, CA: Sensory Integration International. (310-320-9986), 13 pages, $2.00.

Building Productive Futures for Children: An Introduction to Sensory Integration (Video). Torrence, CA: Sensory Integration International. $59.00.

What to Expect from Your 1–3 Year Old by Arlene Eisenberg, Sandee Hathaway, and Heidi Murkoff, 1993, New York: Workman. $10.95.

Touchpoints: Your Child's Emotional and Behavioral Development by T. Berry Brazelton, 1992, Reading, MA: Addison-Wesley.

Understanding My Signals: Help for Parents of Premature Infants by Brenda Hussey-Garder, 1988, Palo Alto, CA: VORT Corporation.

RESOURCES FOR PROFESSIONALS

Temperament in Clinical Practice by Stella Chess and Alexander Thomas, 1995, New York: Guilford Press. (800-365-7006), 315 pages, $19.95.

Infants and Toddlers: A Resource Guide for Practioners by Michael Bender and Carol Ann Baglin, 1992, San Diego, CA: Singular.

The Emotional Life of the Toddler by Alicia F. Liberman, 1993, New York: The Free Press. $22.95.

Developmental Programming for Infants and Young Children by D. Sue Schafer and Martha Moersch, (Eds.), 1981, Ann Arbor, MI: The University of Michigan Press.

Early Intervention for Infants and Children with Handicaps: An Empirical Base by Samuel Odom and Merle Karnes, 1988, Baltimore, MD: Paul H. Brookes. (800-638-3775), 336 pages, $37.00.

Implementing Early Intervention: From Reseach to Effective

Practice by Donna Bryant and Mimi Graham, (Eds.), 1993, Guilford Publications. 358 pages, $32.85.

Handbook of Infant Mental Health by Charles H. Zeanah, (Ed.), 1993, Guilford Publications. 501 pages, $56.95.

Diagnostic Classification of Mental Health and Development Disorders of Infancy and Early Childhood by Stanley Greenspan and Serena Weider, (Eds.), 1994, Alexandria, VA: Zero to Three/National Center for Clinical Infant Programs.

REFERENCES

Broughton, R. J. (1968). Sleep disorders: Disorders of arousal? *Science, 159*, 1070.

Burg, C., Hart, D., Quinn, P., & Rapoport, J. (1978). Newborn minor physical anomalies and prediction of infant behavior. *Journal of Autism and Childhood Schizophrenia, 8*, 427–439.

Carey, W. B. (1970). A simplified method for measuring infant temperament. *Journal of Pediatrics, 77*, 188–194.

Carey, W. B. (1972a). Measuring infant temperament. *Journal of Pediatrics, 81*, 414.

Carey, W. B. (1972b). Clinical applications of infant temperament measurements. *Journal of Pediatrics, 81*, 823–828.

Carey, W. B. (1973). Measurement of infant temperament in pediatric practice. In J. C. Westman (Ed.), *Individual differences in children*. New York: Wiley.

Carey, W. B. (1974). Night waking and temperament in infancy. *Journal of Pediatrics, 84*, 756–758.

Carey, W. B. (1985). Clinical use of temperament data in pediatrics. *Journal of Developmental and Behavioral Pediatrics, 6*, 137–142.

Carey, W. B., Fox, M., & McDevitt, S. C. (1977). Temperament as a factor in early school adjustment. *Pediatrics, 60*, 621–624.

Carey, W. B., & McDevitt S. C. (1978). Revision of the Infant Temperament Questionnaire. *Pediatrics, 61*, 735–739.

DeGangi, G. A. (1991). Assessment of sensory, emotional, and attentional problems in regulatory disordered infants: Part 1. *Infants and Young Children, 3*, 1–8.

DeGangi, G. A. (1993). Prevalence of problems in regulatory disordered sample. *Developmental Dialogue Newsletter*, Reginald Lourie Center, 4, 2.

DeGangi, G. A. (1995). *The test of attention in infants.* Dayton, OH: Southpaw Enterprises.

DeGangi, G. A., Craft, P., & Castellan, J. (1991). Treatment of sensory, emotional and attentional problems in regulatory disordered infants: Part 2. *Infants and Young Children 3*, 9–19.

DeGangi, G. A., DiPietro, J. A., Greenspan, S. I., & Porges, S. W. (1991). Psychophysiological characteristics of the regulatory disordered infant. *Infant Behavior and Development, 14*, 37–50.

DeGangi, G. A., & Greenspan, S. I. (1988). The development of sensory functioning in infants. *Physical and Occupational Therapy in Pediatrics, 8*, 21–33.

DeGangi, G. A., & Greenspan, S. I. (1989). *The test of sensory function in infants.* Los Angeles, CA: Western Psychological Services.

DeGangi, G. A., Poisson, S., Sickel, R. Z., & Wiener, A. S. (1995). *Infant/toddler symptom checklist: A screening tool for parents.* Tucson, AZ: Therapy Skill Builders.

DeGangi, G. A., Porges, S. W., Sickel, R. Z., & Greenspan, S. I. (1993). Four-year follow-up of a sample of regulatory disordered infants. *Infant Mental Health Journal, 4*, 330–343.

Denhoff, E., Hainsworth, P. K., & Hainsworth, M. L. (1972). The child at risk for learning disorder: Can he be identified during the first year of life? *Clinical Pediatrics, 11*, 164–170.

Earls, F. (1981). Temperament characteristics and behavior problems in three-year-old children. *Journal of Nervous and Mental Disease, 169*, 367–373.

Fitzharding, P. M., & Steven, E. M. (1972). The small-for-date infant: Neurological and intellectual sequelae. *Pediatrics, 50*, 50–57.

Forsyth, B., & Canny, P. F. (1991). Perceptions of vulnerability 3½ years after problems of feeding and crying behavior in early infancy. *Pediatrics, 88*, 757–763.

Fullard, W., McDevitt, S. C., & Carey, W. B. (1984). Assessing temperament in one- to three-year-old children. *Journal of Pediatric Psychology, 9*, 205–216.

Greenspan, S. I. (1981). *Psychopathology and adaptation in in-*

fancy and early childhood: Principles of clinical diagnosis and preventive intervention. New York: International Universities Press.

Greenspan, S. I., & Porges, S. W. (1983). Psychopathology in infancy and early childhood: Clinical perspectives on the organization of sensory and affective-thematic experience. *Child Development, 55,* 49–70.

Hoy, E. A., Bell, J. M., & Sykes, D. H. (1988). Very low birth weight: A long-term developmental impairment? *International Journal of Behavioral Development, 11,* 37–67.

Infant Health and Development Program. (1990). Enhancing the outcome of low-birth-weight, premature infants: A multisite, randomized trial. *Journal of the American Medical Association, 263,* 3035–3042.

Kagan, J. (1970). Attention and psychological change in the young child. *Science, 17,* 826–831.

Kagan, J., & Moss, H. A. (1962). *Birth to maturity.* New York: Wiley.

Klebanov, P. K., Brooks-Gunn, J., & McCormick, M. C. (1994). Classroom behavior of very low birth weight elementary school children. *Pediatrics, 94,* 700–708.

Knobloch, H., & Pasamanick, B. (1962). The developmental behavioral approach to the neurologic examination in infancy. *Child Development, 33,* 181.

Lewis, M. (1971). Individual differences in the measurement of early cognitive growth. In J. Hellmuth (Ed.), *Exceptional infant, Vol. 2: Studies in abnormalities* (pp. 172–210). New York: Brunner/Mazel.

Lewis, M. (1975). The development of attention and perception in the infant and young child. In W. M. Cruickshank & D. Hallahan (Eds.), *Perceptual and learning disabilities in children, Vol. 2: Research and theory.* Syracuse, NY: Syracuse University Press.

Lubchenco, L. O., Bard, H., Goldman, A. L., et al. (1975). Newborn intensive care and long-term prognosis. *Developmental Medicine and Child Neurology, 17,* 2–10.

McCormick, M. C., Brooks-Gunn, J., Workman-Daniels, K., Turner, J., & Peckham, G. J. (1992). The health and developmental status of very-low-birth-weight children at school age. *Journal of the American Medication Association, 276,* 2204–2208.

McCormick, M. C., Gortmaker, S. L., & Sobol, A. M. (1990). Very low birth weight children: Behavior problems and school difficulties in a national sample. *Journal of Pediatrics, 117,* 687–693.

Minde, K., Webb, G., & Sykes, D. (1968). Studies on the hyperactive child: VII. *Developmental Medicine and Child Neurology, 10,* 355.

Nichamin, S. (1972). Recognizing minimal cerebral dysfunction in the infant and toddler. *Clinical Pediatrics, 11,* 255–257.

Nichols, P. (1980). Early antecedents of hyperactivity. *Neurology, 30,* 439.

Oberklaid, F., Sanson, A., Pedlow, R., & Prior, M. (1993). Predicting preschool behavior problems from temperament and other variables in infancy. *Pediatrics, 91,* 113–120.

Pasamanick, B. (1974). Minimal brain dysfunction. In H. Knobloch & B. Pasamanick (Eds.), *Gesell and Amatruda's developmental diagnosis.* New York: Harper & Row.

Pasamanick, B., Rogers, M., & Lilienfeld, A. (1956). Pregnancy experience and the development of behavior disorder in children. *American Journal of Psychiatry, 112,* 613–619.

Quinn, P. O., & Rapoport, J. L. (1974). Minor physical anomalies and neurologic status in hyperactive boys. *Pediatrics, 53,* 742–747.

Quinn, P. O., Renfield, M., Burg, C., & Rapoport, J. L. (1977). Minor physical anomalies: A newborn screening and one-year follow-up. *Journal of the American Academy of Child Psychiatry, 16,* 662–669.

Rapoport, J. L., & Quinn, P. O. (1975). Minor physical anomalies (stigmata) and early developmental deviation: A major biological subgroup of "hyperactive children." *The International Journal of Mental Health, 4,* 29–45.

Rosenberg, J. B., & Weller, G. M. (1973). Minor physical anomalies and academic performance in young school children. *Developmental Medicine and Child Neurology, 15,* 131–135.

Ross, G., Lipper, E., & Auld, P. (1990). Social competence and behavior problems in premature children at school age. *Pediatrics, 86,* 391–397.

Rutter, M. (1982). Syndromes attributed to "minimal brain dysfunction" in childhood. *American Journal of Psychiatry, 139,* 21–33.

Rutter, M., Birch, H., Thomas, A., & Chess, S. (1964). Temperamental characteristics in infancy and the later development of behavioral disorders. *British Journal of Psychiatry, 110,* 651–661.

Schaefer, E. S., & Bayley, N. (1963). Maternal behavior, child behavior and their correlations from infancy to adolescence. *Monograph Society for Reasearch and Child Development, 87:*28, no.3.

Schexnider, V. Y. R., Bell, R. Q., Shebilske, W. L., & Quinn, P. (1981). Habituation of visual attention in infants with minor physical anomalies. *Child Development, 52,* 812–818.

Schleifer, M., Weiss, G., Cohen, N., et al. (1975). Hyperactivity in preschoolers and the effect of methylphenidate. *American Journal of Orthopsychiatry, 45,* 38–50.

Smith, A. C., Flick, G. L., Ferriss, G. S., & Sellman, A. H. (1972). Prediction of developmental outcome at seven years from prenatal, perinatal, and postnatal events. *Child Development, 43,* 495–507.

Steg, J. P., & Rapoport, J. L. (1975). Minor physical anomalies in normal, neurotic, learning disabled, and severely disturbed children. *Journal of Autism and Childhood Schizophrenia, 5,* 299–307.

Thomas, A., & Chess, S. (1977). *Temperament and development.* New York: Brunner/Mazel.

Thomas, A., Chess, S., & Birch, H. G. (1968). *Temperament and behavior disorders in children.* New York: New York University Press.

Waldrop, M. F., Bell, R. Q., McLaughlin, B., & Halverson, C. F. (1978). Newborn minor physical anomalies predict short attention span, peer aggression, and impulsivity at age 3. *Science, 199,* 563–564.

Waldrop, M., & Halverson, C. E. (1971). Minor physical anomalies and hyperactive behavior in young children. In J. Hellmuth (Ed.), *The exceptional infant* (pp. 343–381). New York: Brunner/Mazel.

Waldrop, M., Pedersen, F., & Bell, R. (1968). Minor physical anamolies and behavior in preschool children. *Child Development, 39,* 391–400.

Wasserman, R., DiBlasio, C., Bond, L., et al. (1990). Infant temperament and school age behavior: Six-year longitudinal study in a pediatric practice. *Pediatrics, 85,* 801–807.

Weiss, G., & Hechtman, L. (1986). *Hyperactive children grown up*. New York: Guilford Press.

Wender, P. (1971). *Minimal brain dysfunction in children*. New York: Wiley Interscience.

Werner, E., Bierman, J. M., French, F. E., & Simonian, K. (1968). Reproductive and environmental casualties: A report on the 10-year follow-up of the children of the Kauai pregnancy study. *Pediatrics, 42,* 112.

Werry, J. S. (1972). Organic factors in childhood psychopathology. In H. C. Quay & J. S. Werry (Eds.), *Psychopathological disorders of childhood*. New York: Wiley.

Wolff, S. (1967). The contribution of obstetric complications to the etiology of behavior disorders in childhood. *Journal of Child Psychology and Psychiatry, 8,* 57–61.

Chapter 3

THE PRESCHOOL CHILD WITH ADD

If addressing attentional deficits in the infant and toddler is to be perceived as challenging, diagnosing ADD in preschoolers, ages 2 to 5 years, becomes particularly problematic. One of the vital characteristics of this developmental stage is being active. Indeed, we as clinicians worry about the child who is not engaging and exploring his or her environment or who appears to be solitary or withdrawn.

At this time, assessing the quality of the activity level appears to be the best way to make a determination as to whether it is truly a symptom of ADD or merely overactivity in a normal child. If "hyperactivity" is defined as *purposeless* motor activity, it becomes easier to separate out certain behaviors as problematic. The "overactive" child may be running around and playing with great animation, but all these behaviors appear to have a purpose and to fit into some overall "game plan" or the scheme of things. A hyperactive child may simply be running around or wandering from activity to activity, never becoming engaged in any one thing.

According to early reports on this topic, it is the young child's quality and degree of deviant behavior that is the crucial factor in distinguishing him or her from normal, naturally energetic and exuberant peers (Nichamin, 1972). In addition to an analysis and quantification of present activity levels, the same behavioral clues seen in infancy can be helpful in evaluating the clinical significance of any disruptive, inappropriate behavior of the preschool child.

Is there excessive motor activity or aggression? Does the child have particular difficulty with transitions? Do certain textures or types of clothing bother this child, or is tactile defensiveness reported? Are sleep disturbances present? Is the child difficult to console or does he or she overreact out of proportion in a given situation? Are aggressivity and/or tantrums unprovoked? Does the child crave movement? Does he or she engage in risk taking or dangerous behaviors? Are there problems with eating or toileting? Is the child fearful or withdrawn?

Younger children tend to exhibit higher activity levels than older children diagnosed with ADD, and their behaviors may be more situational. Symptoms may not be as pervasive in preschoolers and may occur more at home than at school (Coleman et al., 1977). Some children cannot be distinguished except in structured play situations in school, where they are rated as more active and aggressive. In a nursery population, observations during a free play period did not differentiate between hyperactives and normals. However, in a more structured play situation, "up and away" behaviors and aggressivity did differentiate the hyperactive group (Schleifer et al., 1975).

For boys, overactivity at age 3 years and for girls shyness and difficulty separating were significantly correlated with later behavioral problems at school at age 5 (Coleman et al., 1977). Studies also indicate that ratings of task-oriented behaviors in preschool and the early grades appeared to correlate with later academic competence and achievement (Digman, 1972; Kohn & Rosman, 1974). In a study of 3-year-olds conducted by Richman and coworkers (1975), there was a significant association between problem behavior and poor rapport and task orientation. The problem group also had a tendency to be more active and fidgety and to show extremes of mood (Richman et al., 1975). Prediction of hyperactivity for boys during the early school years was possible from the preschool period but not from infancy. However, males who were hyperactive as infants continued to be significantly more hyperactive than their peers during the preschool period (Battle & Lacey, 1972).

PREVALENCE OF BEHAVIOR PROBLEMS

The incidence of ADD in this age group appears to be similar to that in older children and adolescents. Studies indicate that approximately 7% of a total population of 3-year-olds had moderate to severe behavior problems and 15% had mild behavior problems. Some specific gender differences were found. Boys were rated as more active and to have more enuresis and encopresis. Girls were more fearful than boys, although there was no other sex difference in the frequency of behavior problems (Richman et al., 1975).

In general, activity levels in children were not found to be related to parenting styles but rather to be the result of a genetic predisposition. Correlations between parental attitudes toward child rearing and activity levels of their children was generally not significant (Chamberlain, 1974; Willerman & Plomin, 1973), although parents of active boys tended to be less protective and indulgent. There was, however, a significant correlation between the activity level in the child and the activity level of the parents, which would be consistent with a heritable component to activity level (Willerman & Plomin, 1973).

MINOR PHYSICAL ANOMALIES AND PROBLEM BEHAVIORS AT AGE THREE

Studies of newborn minor physical anomalies and their relationship to problem behaviors at age three report a significant correlation between MPAs and a cluster of behaviors commonly labeled as hyperactive. Waldrop and associates reported a significant association between high newborn anomaly scores and nursery school measures of inattentive, hyperactive behavior for 23 boys. These young boys were observed in two separate free play situations, in a playroom with toys and in a room where there were no toys but the children were free to run around and interact. Data analysis of behavior measures indicated that the higher anomaly boys were more aggressive, impulsive, and had a shorter attention span (Waldrop et al., 1978). In another study, Burg and coworkers found that parents of high anomaly infants were more likely to report problem behaviors at follow-up, when these children were 3 years old, particularly hyperactive-impulsive behavior for boys. Preschool teachers' ratings of hyperactivity, however, did not show a significant relationship to anomaly score (Burg et al., 1980).

DIAGNOSIS OF THE PRESCHOOL CHILD WITH ADD

According to Goldstein in his article "Young Children at Risk: Recognizing the Early Signs of ADHD," the majority of children diagnosed with ADHD could have been diagnosed as toddlers and all by the age of 4 years (Goldstein, 1993). Approximately 95% of children with ADD will have been diagnosed by age 6. Some 30% of children with ADD will be rated as difficult and demanding in infancy, with another 40% diagnosed as hyperactive or inattentive by age 3 or 4 years. Thus, more than 70% of children receiving the diagnosis of ADD will have been identified by the age of 4 years. An additional 20% will be diagnosed in kindergarten or first grade.

Assessments of multiple developmental factors including temperament, social/emotional maturation, attention, and language, motor, and cognitive measures are valuable in making the diagnosis at this stage. Visual processing, sequencing and memory abilities, and spatial/body awareness are likewise important (Dworkin & Levine, 1980).

Preschool children with hyperactivity and attention deficits may be at risk for other problem behaviors as well. Accidents have long been the leading cause of death among preschool children. In numerous studies, children with ADD have been found to be more "accident prone." In one prospective study, twins with more accidents were found to be more active, temperamental, and less attentive. Of all the behavioral variables, the amount of general activity was most strongly related to accident frequency (Matheny et al., 1971, 1972).

In order to diagnose ADD properly at this developmental stage, the clinician must rely on the observation of behaviors in different settings. This includes reports from home, caregivers, and preschool staff. The following story portrays the behaviors exhibited by my patient, Tom, which led to his diagnosis of ADHD. It is told by his mother, Joyce.

> After several years of infertility, three miscarriages, and adoption of our beautiful and wonderful daughter, Margaret I became pregnant with our son Tom. It was a high-risk pregnancy due to the previous miscarriages, so after I went through a cervical closure, I was confined to the house on bed rest from week 13 to delivery. The preg-

nancy and delivery were both normal and Tom arrived three weeks early during a full moon.

When Tom was an infant he used to head bang on our bed, face first. We thought it was strange but he seemed to derive some comfort from it, some kind of soothing sensation. He continued this banging into his high chair, where he would rock rhythmically, banging his head and back against the back of the chair. Sometimes he would take two feet off the floor. I was concerned about any damage he would do to himself, so I got a thick high chair pad to line the seat and back and inserted a pillow behind him to lessen the momentum and force of the bang.

When he could stand, he liked to bang his body at about chest level against the side of his crib. He banged the crib often enough to loosen the screws that held the sides and ends together. We, of course, moved the bumper pads from around the mattress up to the top of the crib rail so that when he was banging himself against the rails he wasn't hurting himself.

Tom was climbing on everything before he could walk. I could never take my eyes off of him. He was unbelievably fast. It was no problem for him to hoist himself over the side of the crib, onto the floor and out of his room. We put up a gate hoping it would keep him confined, but he learned to push his feet against the center of it to bow it out into the shape of a "C" and squeeze through. Then we got another gate and placed it on top of the first gate, so that he couldn't get his hands on top of the bottom gate or use any body leverage to escape. His door frame was beginning to look a lot like jail.

Once I asked a friend to watch him while he was in his walker while I got dressed to go out for dinner. Before she knew it, he had reached into a lower kitchen cabinet, pulled out a few serving pieces, rolled into the next door laundry room, pulled out all of the clothes in the dryer, zoomed out of the kitchen, across the dining room and living room, into a bedroom, and finally into the bathroom where he threw everything into the toilet. She was amazed at his speed and agility.

We found that Tom didn't like to take naps every day like his sister did. She always went to naptime easily just about 2 P.M. every day for two hours. He couldn't do that. I would put him in his room, he'd be very tired, but he couldn't stop moving. He would destroy his room because he didn't want to be there. One day, he pulled out a couple of drawers in his dresser, climbed up them like a ladder, and sat in the top drawer. Unfortunately, it fell over on him. Luckily he was unhurt. At this point, our pediatrician said that he was one of those kids who didn't nap every day, probably every third day, and that I would have to get used to it. Also, Tom didn't have to sleep in his bed and that sleeping on the couch in the playroom was okay. He did like to sleep in the car, though; the motion would usually put him to sleep, and he'd stay asleep until we stopped to get out.

One Friday morning, he was behaving particularly badly. I was at my wit's end. I had already spanked him five times and timed him out 10 times when I decided that he hadn't had enough sleep, that he was overtired, and that he needed to go back to bed. This was about 8:30 A.M. He was screaming and crying, just generally making a nuisance of himself. So I got him back in bed, waited outside of his room for five minutes, heard that it was quiet, and went downstairs to the office to return a phone call.

About two minutes later, I heard a loud "thwack" and then crying. Not recognizing the sound, I hung up and went out to look for what happened. There I found Tom crying on the floor of our living room/great room. [The room has a cathedral ceiling.] He had squeezed through the second-floor railing pickets overlooking our living room and fallen, breaking the stairway banister off the wall, bounced off the steps, and landed on the rug. I honestly didn't know whether to cry or be mad. After getting angry at him, spanking him, telling him how dangerous that was to go out there, because he liked to squeeze through and sit on the 6-inch ledge, he did the very same thing the next day, and a few more times before we figured out a way to block it off.

When he was 2½, I put him in preschool three mornings a week. I really needed a break, and this seemed like a great solution. There was another child in his class, also with undiagnosed ADHD, who was incredibly aggressive, hyper, and impulsive. Tom, on the other hand, was not aggressive, but was hyper and impulsive. He also didn't talk as much as his sister, who, from 18 months on, never stopped talking. Tom was a boy of few words. He did, however, say "John pushed me" one day. Unfortunately, Tom and John had been paired together as the two children in the class with behavioral problems. We thought this unfair because our son was not half as bad or wild as the other child. Even so, Tom was labeled as a suspected ADHD behavior problem and we got the accompanying preconceived attitude that your kid is a problem and will always be a pain. But Tom is actually smart, very sweet, affectionate, and extremely sensitive.

One day on the way home from school, Tom fell asleep in the car. I carefully carried him inside and put him down on the couch in the playroom, hoping he would sleep for awhile. I then went to return a friend's phone call. When I got off the phone, I went to check on him and he was nowhere to be found. I asked my daughter where he was and she said that he went outside. He couldn't get the doors open at this time, so she had let him out. I went outside and looked around and couldn't see him anywhere. This was really scary because we live on 5½ acres, and there's a partially filled pond behind our property, woods to the right rear, and undeveloped land across the street.

After calling for him several times with no answer and thinking I'll never find him like this and I'll have to call the police for a helicopter, my daughter and I got in the car and went flying down the driveway. Halfway down, I looked over to the right at my neighbor's front field, and there's Tom, standing under one of their horses between its hind legs playing with its tail.

"Come on Tom. Time to go home!" I yelled. "No!" he said. Of course. So I offered him a cookie and he walked right over to me. Thank God.

The following year, we put Tom in a preschool morning program that I thought was strictly nursery. Unfortunately, over the summer, they had changed the curriculum. The director of the school found that Tom couldn't handle it, that he was overstimulated by the amount of activity going on in the room, and by the number of students in the class (20). He would stand by himself and wring his hands. Other ADHD children often become aggressive and push, but that was not Tom's reaction.

The director of the school would remove him from the class, bring him into her office, and let him play with her magic wand and be with her. Here we were paying tuition so that he could sit in her office. By November, we had a conference with the school director and three of the school staff who had dealt with Tom.

They recommended that we get him tested for ADHD. We were upset because we didn't want our son to have to have any problems in life and ADHD seemed like such a terrible thing to have. I was sad that our son wasn't perfect and very fearful of what was ahead for us.

They also told me I was treating Tom like a first child, and that wasn't right. I still don't understand that to this day. I would actually think that was a good thing because most first children get a lot of attention, usually more than succeeding children. Anyway, I ended up feeling guilty and that I was doing something wrong in my parenting.

Anyway, we had him tested by a psychologist a few weeks later, who said she suspected that he had ADHD, that his hyperactivity was interfering with his ability to take the test, and that we needed to see a developmental pediatrician.

By then we had changed Tom's school, which is no easy thing to do midyear. We put him in a morning nursery program four days a week. It turned out to be a disaster. His teacher was so ill informed about ADHD that she treated Tom like he was a real brat. She'd had previous experience with another boy at a former school, so she expected the same behavior from Tom. She didn't know what she was doing, she was nasty, and she made him feel like he was a problem, so he lived up to her expectation. She discouraged any friendships from developing between him and any of the other students by whispering about him to me in front of their parents. She did more damage in a short time than any teacher or school so far.

During this time, medication had been prescribed for Tom on a daily basis. His teacher was to rate him daily on behavior forms so that we could track the effect of his medication. He started out on Ritalin (methylphenidate) which did not agree with him at all. We found him to be very uptight, cold, and irritable. The doctor took him off everything and started him on low doses of Dexedrine (dextroamphetamine). That has worked for Tom and continues to be effective today. The doctor also recommended occupational therapy for development of fine motor skills because Tom found it difficult to hold a pencil correctly and to color.

After a complete and thorough evaluation, Tom was diagnosed with ADHD with associated learning disabilities of language processing and auditory lag, which would explain why his speech was delayed and his inability to express himself. Initially, we had reservations about putting our son on medication. However, after we learned that ADHD is a neurological problem, and that medication helps turn on parts of the brain that aren't turned on, and slows down the impulses coming from the cortex causing the hyperactivity, we felt it would be more beneficial than not to put him on it and that we'd have to get over our fear.

His behavior is like night and day when he's on medication and when he's not. My husband had reservations because he is a recovering alcoholic, and he was worried about addiction problems with the medication, or any untoward effect it might have on Tom, because alcoholism is sometimes hereditary. But so far, it seems to be working pretty well. It's made all the difference in his demeanor and attitude toward school, life, and so on.

The following year we put Tom in a 3-day morning preschool program with small class size and traditional nursery. Again, we ran up against the ignorance of the teaching profession in dealing with children with ADHD, or when they hear the term, your kid is immediately labeled as a behavior problem. This time I didn't tell them anything when he started because I refused to let them label him.

About a month after school started, the teacher called and was concerned because Tom would never eat the snack with the rest of the class, and she wanted to know if he was allergic to anything or what the problem was. So I spilled the beans and told her it was a side effect from the medication and not to worry about it. Then we started to get complaints that he was making faces at the other children, that they were being put off by his behavior, and they didn't like him because they didn't think that he liked them. It went on and on.

By the end of the year, we met with our developmental pediatrician, who had suggested we test Tom for kindergarten readiness. He was evaluated by an educational consultant and retested to assess developmental progress. This time he did much better on the tests, thanks to the effectiveness of the medication and growing up a little bit more.

As a result of the testing, a year of special education was recommended. We were upset because we had three options at this point and were worried about making the wrong decision. We could leave him in the school he was at to attend an afternoon class with 5-year-olds, who were old enough for kindergarten but not ready; put him in a private kindergarten and hope that he could swing it; or try for the very-hard-to-get-into special education pre-academic kindergarten. We opted for door number 3 and started the process with the school system, which was really involved.

We got Tom evaluated by the school psychologist who told me I had to let go and that my anxiety about him would affect him and that he would be fine. Then we had him tested by a speech pathologist, gathered up all our previous evaluations and recommendations, got in touch with our home-school pupil personnel worker, and submitted our application for a spot in the program for Tom. We then got a date for our interview with the school system's Application Review Board, where Tom was assigned a code for ADHD and a code for his learning disabilities. In addition the degree of services to be rendered was decided.

Lucky for us they put him in the program. It has been the best school year ever for Tom. His teacher is fantastic, and so are the associated staff who work with him in speech pathology and other services. He's at the top of the heap for the first time. He's developed self-esteem in school, something that was always questionable before.

He's been mainstreamed into the regular kindergarten classroom, and he's had no problem with class size (31) or with the work. Hopefully when he is mainstreamed into our home school next year, he'll do as well.

It's very worthwhile to become familiar with your school system's resources for special education and to learn how the system operates. The services our son has received this year would have cost us hundreds of dollars if we were to have paid for them privately. It's worth the effort to pursue the process because at least where we live, once you're in the system, you can tailor the services your child needs as you go along, using the system to your maximum advantage.

As a sidebar to this story, my husband has learned a great deal about himself from Tom. He has been diagnosed with ADHD in the last year and is also on medication. He says looking at Tom is like looking at himself when he was a child, except that our son has self-esteem and is happy. My husband's parents had a hard time handling him and mismanaged the problem. They did not know anything about ADHD.

We are so fortunate to have found out about Tom early. The medication and other recommendations have made such a difference in our son's behavior. Our family was becoming very dysfunctional. We found we couldn't control Tom and were resorting to spanking too often to handle the behavior, and we didn't want our parenting to be like that. We felt we were encouraging violent behavior. We also felt it unfair to our daughter that we were having to spend so much time managing Tom's behavior that we were neglecting her. Our house was out of balance, and we needed to get some control.

Currently Tom still head bangs on his pillow when he's trying to get back to sleep. He's still difficult to manage and requires much more patience than either one of us ever thought we had. We have learned to deal with him differently from how we deal with our daughter, that he takes more effort, and that we can't engage in head-to-head confrontation but can go around sideways or around back to get what we want from him. But if that's what it takes, that's okay. I wouldn't trade him for anything in the world. He's a great kid.

EVALUATION OF TODDLERS FOR ADD

During the interview with the parents, the clinician must be sensitive to those factors that predispose to difficulties, as so unforgettably described in the above presentation and discussed in the previous chapter. The pediatrician or health care professional should have been alerted by several factors that placed Tom "at risk" for developmental and behavioral issues. These included the infertility and previous miscarriages, which made for a "high-risk" pregnancy. Early sensory integration problems and a regulatory disorder were manifested by Tom's head-banging and sleep issues. He gave up naps early and did not sleep or settle down for very long periods. He was difficult to handle and his parents felt overwhelmed, even though this was their second child. Also noteworthy were Tom's frequent accidents and injuries. When he entered nursery school at age two, other problems surfaced. He was reported to have delayed expressive language skills and had difficulty adjusting to preschool. In addition to the above factors, there was a positive family history for ADHD in Tom's father and grandfather. When all of these facts were considered together Tom was certainly "at risk." By attending to symptoms and following the diagnostic process, Tom's ADHD and language-based developmental problems were diagnosed before age four, allowing for early intervention and multimodal treatment.

COMPONENTS OF THE DIAGNOSTIC PROCESS

The diagnosis of ADD in this age group relies heavily on historical facts and subjective information obtained from interviews with parents and school personnel. Important factors in the past history include obstetric or perinatal complications and a health history that may be positive for illnesses or conditions that predispose to ADD. These latter include central nervous system infections (meningitis, encephalitis), failure to thrive, anemia, lead intoxication, and frequent ear infections. Early developmental milestones should also be documented as some, but not all, children have concurrent developmental delays.

A physical examination—including measurement of head circumference, minor physical anomalies, and neuromaturational levels—should be performed. A vision and hearing screen is indicated for all preschoolers but especially those with evidence of hyperactivity and language delays. Neurodevelopmental screening and psychoeducational testing should also be performed on all children to rule out developmental delays and establish cognitive and learning styles.

Direct observations of the child by the clinician in a structured play situation should also be conducted. This can be performed in the office setting to assess ability to attend, follow directions, and cooperate. However, task orientation, aggressivity, attention span, distractibility, and activity level can be observed more accurately in the preschool environment than in a one-to-one setting. If this is not feasible, then a discussion with the child's preschool teacher or caretaker may suffice. It is important to seek out these independent observations of the child, as sometimes parents have a narrow frame of reference on which to judge their child's behavior. In my office, I once saw an extremely hyperactive 3-year-old, whose mother had few complaints. She was coping very nicely by taking her son outdoors to the park all day to let him play. She made few demands, and as long as he was allowed to run and climb in this unstructured setting, he was fine. It was only upon entering preschool that problems began.

RATING SCALES AND QUESTIONNAIRES

Behavior rating scales are also available for the preschool child. One of the newer scales is *The Early Childhood Attention Deficit Disorder Evaluation Scale* (ECADDES) published by Hawthorne Educational Services (McCarney, 1995). This scale is designed to be used with children 24 through 72 months of age and uses the descriptors provided by DSM-IV and the most currently recognized subclassifications. It has both a school version (56 items) and a home version (50 items) for reporting parent input, which can be completed in approximately 15 minutes. A home version of the scale is now available in Spanish. The standardization sample included 5,041 children from all geographic regions of the United States, which included 30 states. The Intervention Manual, which accompanies this scale, includes goals and objectives for an IEP as well as intervention strategies for teachers who work with ADHD children either in special education or regular education settings (McCarney & Johnson, 1995).

Behar and Stringfield (1974) have previously developed their *Preschool Behavior Questionnaire* that can be used as a screening instrument by mental health professionals to assess preschoolers who show symptoms or a constellation of symptoms that suggest emerging emotional problems. It has been used over the years in both clinical and research settings as a first step in the diagnosis of behavior problems. Teachers fill out the questionnaire using a 3-point scale to rate the child on 30 items. Three factors were found to be significant. These were Factor I, which measures hostile-aggressive behaviors; Factor II, which isolates anxious-fearful traits; and Factor III, which is characterized by poor attention span and restlessness and appears to measure hyperactive-distractible behaviors.

Bell, Waldrop, and Weller (1972), likewise, devised a rating system for the assessment of hyperactive and withdrawn preschool children. With it, six aspects of hyperactivity and three of withdrawal can be rated on a weekly basis by the preschool teachers on an 11-point scale. These ratings are then converted to two-factor scores. This system is valuable when used in the clinical setting to identify children with these particular characteristics or to evaluate response to treatment intervention.

The Toddler Temperament Scale and the Carey Revised Infant Temperament Questionnaire, discussed in Chapter 2, are also particularly useful for assessing the preschool child. These scales allow for diagnosis of difficult temperament and may be used by the clinician to facilitate counseling and to assist in parental adjustment or environmental changes (Blondis, Accardo, & Snow, 1989).

MULTIMODAL TREATMENT PROGRAMS

Parent education regarding the symptoms of ADD as they present in this age group and support for handling their preschooler with attentional deficits, impulsivity, and/or hyperactivity is critical. The stresses that accompany raising a child with ADD combined with the normal developmental issues of need for control and separation can be overwhelming to parents. At this point the mental health professional or physician will need to assist in the process by teaching appropriate parenting skills and behavior management techniques to the parents.

Young children with ADD tend to do best in a highly structured environment. Sometimes this is difficult to achieve, especially if a parent also has ADD. Unknowingly, parents may reinforce the inappropriate or attention-getting behaviors of their toddlers. Parents and caretakers, however, can be taught behavior management techniques to address problem behaviors. Appropriate methods of reinforcement can be used to redirect maladaptive behaviors and reward appropriate ones.

Studies seem to indicate that children identified at this early stage tend to be more hyperactive than children identified later. For cases involving a high level of hyperactivity or impulsivity or when children are dangerous to themselves or others, the use of medication may be indicated. Impulsivity may cause children at this age to engage in more dangerous or "risk-taking" behaviors and become involved in more frequent accidents. Aggressivity and uncontrolled temper outbursts may be present and may negatively affect family or peer relationships. For these children, the use of medication may indeed by lifesaving.

Fewer controlled studies have been performed in this age group regarding the effectiveness of medication. An early study of methylphenidate in a group of preschoolers indicated that although the mothers' complaints about their children decreased while the children were on medication, there was no corroboration of any change from the observations collected from the preschool setting or on psychological testing. Mothers did rate their children as less aggressive and hyperactive at home, but clinical observations indicated that methylphenidate had a negative effect on the child's mood and relationship with peers. Children on medication had less social behavior and interaction with others. Unwanted behaviors included sadness, irritability, excessive clinging and hugging, and increased solitary play. Decreased appetite and difficulty falling asleep at night were also reported (Schleifer et al., 1975).

The effects of methylphenidate on the interactions of preschool children with ADD and their mothers were also studied. Interaction problems are reported especially in 4- and 5-year-olds (Mash & Johnson, 1982). In a study of children ranging in age from 2 years 7 months to 4 years 11 months, Barkley (1988) reported that medication at a low dose had few effects on mother–child interaction in the free play situation except that the mother used less direct commands. On a higher dose, the children with ADD decreased their non-compliant as well as their off-task behavior. The preschoolers also significantly increased their rates of compliance by 15% and the length of sustained compliance to maternal commands during the task period. There was also a trend for mothers to be more rewarding or praising of their children who were on medication, and mothers were more likely to employ questions or general interactive comments instead of commands. More side effects were reported during the medication trial but these did not reach significant levels (Barkley, 1988).

SCHOOL READINESS AND PLACEMENT ISSUES

One of the issues arising frequently during the assessment and treatment of preschool children with developmental delays is the question of their readiness for kindergarten placement. Initial studies demonstrated that a child who was not ready rarely caught up and tended to maintain an uneven pattern of development. This suggested that such a child be given an additional year in which to "catch up" developmentally (Gesell Institute, 1980). Recent research, however, has documented that retention alone is not the best answer to this problem. Children who were "held back" were found to perform below the level of normal controls or children who had not repeated a year in math and reading. When tested at the end of third grade, their full-scale scores were also lower, even though they were chronologically a year older than the other children (May & Welch, 1984).

This theory of allowing another year for development appears to be flawed, as it does not address the individual needs of the child and/or provide a program for intervention and remediation (Niklason, 1984). Transition programs initially appeared to be a viable alternative to simply waiting or repeating a year before kindergarten placement, but any positive results were found to have disappeared by third grade (Gredler, 1984).

Programs that allow the child who is chronologically ready for kindergarten an intensive opportunity for remediation of identified weaknesses appear to be the best solution. Such programs, which address "weaknesses" at the kindergarten level, allow the child to go on to learn basic preacademic skills and to progress in both social and emotional development. These programs can also provide a more structured environment than the preschool setting in which to observe and address attention span and activity level. Research suggests that optimal development occurs as a result of the child's interaction with a stimulating environment, and it is rare that the needs of an "unready" child are met by simply delaying school entry (Black, 1990).

Proper school placement appears to be critical to ensure a positive early learning experience. In choosing a school, it is always important to seek as good a "match" as possible. Placement should always take into account the needs of the individual child. This includes addressing such issues as activity level, degree of disorganization, fine and gross motor development, and need for structure or creativity. The teacher's attitude and education regarding learning differences, the school's philosophy, and teaching styles should all be evaluated. In general, does the teacher appear to be approachable, professional, encouraging, flexible, and organized? Is he or she respectful of the students? What tone of voice is used? What is the overall atmosphere in the classroom and school? (Quinn, 1990).

The physical arrangement as well as the atmosphere of the classroom is also important to ensure success. Attention to some practical suggestions may assist the young child in functioning more comfortably in the classroom. Three factors have been found to be critical when working with the preschool child with ADD. These are: brevity, variety, and structure/routine (Jones, 1989).

Suggestions for managing the learning environment of an

active preschooler include maintaining a setting that is orderly and structured, with lots of labeling and color coding; preferential seating, close to the teacher and in a defined space; individualization of directions; a routine schedule; the use of auditory and visual cues to signal transitions; and supportive feedback. In addition, the classroom should be childproofed to protect the impulsive child (Jones, 1993).

Other individual therapies may be indicated at this stage to address the motor or language delays seen in some children with ADD. Sensory integration deficits may be present in those preschoolers who were noted to be regulatory disordered infants. If symptoms persist into this period, referral for occupational therapy should be made. Psychoeducational assessment to evaluate school readiness is critical not only to address placement issues but also to determine cognitive styles and possible learning disabilities.

CONCLUSION

At this point the child with ADD has entered another stage of development, and his or her world is expanding. In addition to parents and siblings, the child must now deal with teachers and peers. However, this broadening of horizons may lead to additional difficulties. Structured school and play situations, with the need for appropriate social interactions, place added demands on attention and control of behaviors. Aggressivity and an increased activity level interfere to a greater extent in these new settings.

The child with ADD may have coexisting developmental delays and/or be considered at risk for learning problems. Commonly, additional interventions are needed both at home and school. It is the role of the clinicians to be aware of these many needs as the diagnosis of ADD in the preschooler is being entertained. The judicial use of medication, parent education, behavior modification, and other therapies is critical to establishing improved behaviors and a positive educational experience for the preschooler with ADD.

RESOURCES FOR THE CHILD, PARENTS, AND CAREGIVERS

1-2-3 Magic!: Training Your Preschoolers and Preteens to Do What You Want! by Thomas W. Phelan, 1984, Glen Ellyn, IL: Child Management. (800-442-4453), 180 pages, $10.00.

Good Behavior by Stephen Garber, Marianne D. Garber, and Robyn F. Spizman, 1987, New York: Random House. 476 pages, $22.50.

The Parent's Guide to Early Childhood Attention Deficit Disorders Intervention Manual by Stephen B. McCarney and Nancy W. Johnson, 1995, Columbia, MO: Hawthorne Educational Services. (800-542-1673), 134 pages, $13.00.

Shelly the Hyperactive Turtle by Deborah Moss, 1989, Bethesda, MD: Woodbine Press. (800-843-7323), 20 pages, $12.95.

RESOURCES FOR PROFESSIONALS

Behavior Problems in Preschool Children: Clinical and Developmental Issues by Susan Campbell, 1990, New York: Guilford Press. 270 pages, $32.95.

Sourcebook for Children with Attention Deficit Disorder: A Management Guide for Early Childhood Professionals and Parents by Clare Jones, 1991, San Antonio, TX: The Psychological Corporation. (800-228-0752), 184 pages, $35.00.

Early Childhood Attention Deficit Disorder Evaluation Scales (ECADDES) by Stephen McCarney, 1995, Columbia, MO:

Hawthorne Educational Services, plus Intervention Manual, $22.00.

REFERENCES

Barkley, R. A. (1988). The effects of methylphenidate on the interactions of preschool ADHD children with their mothers. *Journal of the American Academy of Child and Adolescent Psychiatry, 27,* 336–341.

Battle, E. S., & Lacey, B. (1972). A context for hyperactivity in children over time. *Child Development, 43,* 757–773.

Behar, L., & Stringfield, S. (1974). A behavior rating scale for the preschool child. *Developmental Psychology, 10,* 601–610.

Bell, R. Q., Waldrop, M. F., & Weller, G. M. (1972). A rating system for the assessment of hyperactive and withdrawn children in preschool samples. *American Journal of Orthopsychiatry, 42,* 23–34.

Black, J. L. (1990). School readiness. *Pediatric Basics,* 2–12.

Blondis, T. A., Accardo, P. J., & Snow, J. H. (1989). Measures of attention, Part I: Questionnaires. *Clinical Pediatrics, 28,* 222–228.

Burg, C., Rapoport, J., Bartley, L., et al. (1980). Newborn minor physical anomalies and problem behavior at age three. *American Journal of Psychiatry, 137,* 791–796.

Chamberlain, R. W. (1974). Authoritarian and accommodative child-rearing styles: Their relationships with the behavior patterns of 2-year-old children and with other variables. *Journal of Pediatrics, 84,* 287–293.

Coleman, J., Wolkind, S., & Ashley, L. (1977). Symptoms of behavior disturbance and adjustment to school. *Journal of Child Psychology and Psychiatry, 18,* 201–209.

Digman, J. M. (1972). High school academic achievement as seen in the context of a longitudinal study of personality. *Proceedings: 80th Annual Convention of the American Psychological Association,* 19–20.

Dworkin, P. H., & Levine, M. D. (1980). The preschool child: prediction and prescription. In A. P. Scheiner & I. F. Abroms

(Eds.), *The practical management of the developmentally disabled child*. St. Louis, MO: Mosby.

Gesell Institute of Human Development. (1980). *A gift of time … A developmental point of view*. New Haven, CT: Author.

Goldstein, S. (1993). Young children at risk: Recognizing the early signs of ADHD. *The ADHD report*. New York: Guilford Press.

Gredler, G. R. (1984). Transition classes: A viable alternative for the at-risk child? *Psychology in the Schools, 21*, 463–470.

Jones, C. B. (1989). Teachers' corner. In *Kids getting you down?* (Newsletter). San Diego, CA: Learning Development Services.

Jones, C. B. (1993). The young and the restless: Helping the preschool child with attention deficit/hyperactivity disorder. *CHADDER*, 13–17.

Kohn, M., & Rosman, B. (1974). Social-emotional, cognitive, and demographic determinants of poor school achievement: Implications for a strategy of intervention. *Journal of Educational Psychology, 66*, 267–276.

Mash, E. J., & Johnson, C. (1982). A comparison of the mother–child interactions of younger and older hyperactive and normal children. *Child Development, 53*, 1371–1381.

Matheny, A. P., Brown, A. M., & Wilson, R. S. (1971). Behavioral antecedents of accidental injuries in early childhood: A study of twins. *Journal of Pediatrics, 79*, 122–124.

Matheny, A. P., Brown, A. M., & Wilson, R. S. (1972). Assessment of children's behavioral characteristics: A tool in accident prevention. *Clinical Pediatrics, 11*, 437–439.

May, D. C., & Welch, E. L. (1984). The effects of developmental placement and early retention on children's later scores on standardized tests. *Psychology in the Schools, 21*, 381–385.

McCarney, S. B. (1995). *The early childhood attention deficit disorders evaluation scale*. Columbia, MO: Hawthorne Educational Services.

McCarney, S. B., & Johnson, N. (1995). *The early childhood attention deficit disorders intervention manual*. Columbia, MO: Hawthorne Educational Services.

Nichamin, S. (1972). Recognizing minimal cerebral dysfunction in the infant and toddler. *Clinical Pediatrics, 11*, 255–257.

Niklason, L. B. (1984). Nonpromotion: A pseudoscientific solution. *Psychology in Schools, 21*, 485–499.

Quinn, P. O. (1990). If your child is ..., then ... In B. Lyons & M. James (Eds.), Choosing the right school for your child: A guide to selected elementary schools in the Washington area. Lanaham, MD: Madison Books.

Richman, N., Stevenson, J. E., & Graham, P. J. (1975). Prevalence of behavior problems in 3-year-old children: An epidemiological study in a London borough. *Journal of Child Psychology and Psychiatry, 16*, 277–287.

Schleifer, M., Weiss, G., Cohen, N., et al. (1975). Hyperactivity in preschoolers and the effect of methylphenidate. *American Journal of Orthopsychiatry, 45*, 38–50.

Waldrop, M., Bell, R., McLaughlin, B., et al. (1978). Newborn minor physical anomalies predict short attention span, peer aggression, and impulsivity at age 3. *Science, 199*, 563–565.

Willerman, L., & Plomin, R. (1973). Activity level in children and their parents. *Child Development, 44*, 854–858.

Chapter 4

THE ELEMENTARY
SCHOOL CHILD

With several thousand papers published on the subject of ADD in the elementary school child, it is quite obvious that this is the group on which the most research has been done and about which the most has been written. This chapter will therefore present only a brief overview of the disorder in this age group.

Like Tom, who was presented in the last chapter, hyperactive youngsters are easy to spot and rarely escape diagnosis in the preschool period. However, the diagnosis of children without hyperactivity or those with predominantly inattentive type can be more difficult and they can evade the best clinicians for years.

Jeff is a sixth-grade student newly diagnosed as having ADD without hyperactivity. He is responding nicely to stimulant medication without side effects and is now doing well at school and is getting along better at home, but this was not always the case.

Jeff's family always considered him "spacey" and "never quite with you." He was impulsive and "in his own dimension." Jeff would frequently show up at home missing his belongings (including his shoes on one occasion) and having no idea where they were. He would characteristically appear in the morning wearing different-colored socks, as he paid little attention to visual details. Mealtimes would usually end in chaos, as did family vacations. Negative interactions between Jeff and his two siblings and exasperation on the part of his parents led to many conflicts at home. Family counseling was attempted when Jeff was age four. "Time out" was tried, but this had no effect on his behaviors. Jeff became overanxious, as he really wanted to please. Redirecting an activity to something more appropriate seemed to work better than anything else. Jeff could concentrate for hours on video games and became the "local expert," although his handwriting and fine motor skills remained poor.

Jeff was reading by kindergarten and was considered "very bright" by his teachers, who recognized his potential. In first grade, once he had finished his work, Jeff was allowed to get up and move around. With motivation, he could "settle" for a period of time. By second grade, he could write stories that were creative and funny. He was musically and athletically talented yet he "marched to the beat of a different drummer." Eventually he "turned off" to reading and the word *hurry* was not in his vocabulary. Time management and organizational problems interfered with academic performance and family relationships. Jeff's work was considered "sloppy" by his teachers and frequent "careless" mistakes lowered his grades on most tests. In class, he tended to "doodle" or "fool around" and talk to the other students. He had difficulty sitting for any length of time to do his homework and was constantly "taking breaks." His assignments were frequently missing or incomplete.

By the end of fifth grade, Jeff's parents and teachers were desperate to find out what was wrong with him. He was referred for a full psychoeducational assessment and diagnosed as having ADD. Instances of missing some of the information presented auditorily and impulsiveness in responses were reported. A relatively weak score was noted on reading comprehension, which was most likely due to inattention and not to a slow reading rate. It was suspected that Jeff had difficulty staying focused on the material and did not process all of the written information.

A trial of stimulant medication was undertaken and proved to be extremely effective. Jeff immediately noticed the difference in his ability to sit and focus and his parents reported improved relationships around the house. Jeff seemed more "on task" and "tuned in."

DIAGNOSIS OF ADD

At the present time, the diagnosis of ADD remains a historical one, relying on the persistent pattern of symptoms of inattention and/or hyperactivity and impulsivity. These symptoms must have been present before the age of 7 years and been reported or observed in at least two settings. They must be severe enough to interfere with developmentally appropriate functioning in either the social or academic settings.

Diagnostic criteria have been set forth in the DSM-IV and include the following symptomatology:

DIAGNOSTIC CRITERIA FOR ATTENTION DEFICIT/HYPERACTIVITY DISORDER*

Inattention. Six or more of the following symptoms that have persisted for at least 6 months:

(a) often fails to give close attention to details or makes careless mistakes in schoolwork, work, or other activities
(b) often has difficulty sustaining attention in tasks or play activities
(c) often does not seem to listen when spoken to directly
(d) often does not follow through on instructions and fails to finish schoolwork, chores, or duties in the workplace (not due to oppositional behavior or failure to understand instructions)
(e) often has difficulties organizing tasks and activities
(f) often avoids, dislikes, or is reluctant to engage in tasks that require sustained mental effort (such as schoolwork or homework)
(g) often loses things necessary for tasks or activities (e.g., toys, school assignments, pencils, books, or tools)
(h) is often distracted by extraneous stimuli
(i) is often forgetful in daily activities

Hyperactivity-impulsivity. Six (or more) of the following symptoms have persisted for at least 6 months:

Hyperactivity:

(a) often fidgets with hands or feet or squirms in seat
(b) often leaves seat in classroom or in other situations in which remaining seated is expected

---

*Reprinted with permission from the *Diagnostic and Statistical Manual of Mental Disorders,* Fourth Edition. Copyright 1994 American Psychiatric Association.

(c) often runs about or climbs excessively in situations in which it is inappropriate (in adolescents or adults may be limited to subjective feelings of restlessness)

(d) often has difficulty playing or engaging in leisure activities quietly

(e) is often "on the go" or often acts as if "driven by a motor"

(f) often talks excessively

Impulsivity:

(g) often blurts out answers before questions have been completed

(h) often has difficulty awaiting turn

(i) often interrupts or intrudes on others (e.g., butts into conversations or games)

As can be seen from the above clustering, the disorder is now characterized as being predominantly of the inattentive type or predominantly of the hyperactive/impulsive type. These types are determined by the characteristics exhibited. An individual can be diagnosed as having symptoms of both types, which is then referred to as combined type. Most children and adolescents with ADD have the combined type of the disorder.

RATING SCALES

Over the past several years numerous rating scales have been developed for use by the clinician to gather information on the student from the classroom teacher as well as the parents. These behavioral checklists have several advantages as well as disadvantages. They certainly are convenient for gathering information and assessing multiple dimensions of behavior. Based on normative data, they provide a tool for assessing the extent of difference between the behavior of the student and his or her peers. However, they cannot on their own diagnose or rule out ADD.

As numerous scales exist, I would like to briefly mention several of the more popular scales at this time and refer the reader to an excellent comparison of the various scales by Kathy Sharp (1993) or a review of questionnaires as measures of attention deficit by Blondis and colleagues (1989) if they seek more indepth information on the subject.

Child Behavioral Checklist (Parent, Teacher, or Youth Forms) (CBCL) by Thomas Achenbach, 1991, Burlington, VT: University of Vermont, Department of Psychiatry. (802-656-4563).

Behavior Assessment System for Children (Parent, Teacher, Self-Report Forms) by Cecil Reynolds and Randy Kamphaus. Circle Pines, MN: American Guidance Service.

Conners Parent and Teacher Questionnaires by C. K. Conners, 1989, North Tonawanda, NY: Multi-Health Systems. (800-456-3003).

Child Symptom Inventories (CSI) by Kenneth Gadow and Joyce Sprafkin, 1994, Stony Brook, NY: Checkmate Plus, Ltd. (516-360-3432).

Attention Deficit Disorders Evaluation Scale (ADDES) by Stephen McCarney, 1995, Columbia, MO: Hawthorne Educational Services. (800-542-1673).

Home and School Situations Questionnaires by Russell Barkley in *Attention-Deficit Hyperactivity Disorder: A Clinical Workbook,* 1991, New York: Guiford Press. (800-365-7006).

ADD Comprehensive Teacher Rating Scale (ACTeRS) by R. Ullmann, E. K. Sleator, and R. L. Sprague, 1991, Champagne, IL: Metritech. (217-398-4868).

Children's Attention and Adjustment Survey (CAAS) by N. Lambert, C. Hartsough, and J. Sandoval, 1990, Palo Alto, CA: Consulting Psychologists Press.

To aid in the diagnosis and treatment of children with ADD it is important that the clinician become familiar with one or several of the scales listed above and consistently use them as part of the assessment process. The use of rating scales not only establishes a baseline during this process but they also assist in quantifying status at follow-up, thus monitoring response to various treatment interventions.

PERSISTENCE OF SYMPTOMS

As discussed in Chapter 1, the symptom of hyperactivity has been found to be relatively stable over time. This was demonstrated in several studies including a prospective follow-up of those children formally diagnosed as having generalized hyperkinesis during a total population screening of 3,448 children conducted in Göteborg, Sweden. All children were screened by preschool teachers when they were 6 years of age. Eighteen children (1%) were formally diagnosed at age 7 years by a multidisciplinary team as having generalized or pervasive hyperkinesis; 29 were diagnosed as having situational attention deficit/hyperkinesis, demonstrating this behavior in two of three examination situations. Fifteen of these 18 children were then followed up, at ages 10 and 13 years.

Of the 15 children with generalized hyperkinesis who were seen at follow-up, 14 were situationally hyperactive at both 10 and 13 years. Eleven of these 14 also fulfilled the criteria for pervasive hyperkinesis at age 10 and 6 at age 13. Four children were diagnosed as having a conduct disorder at follow-up (1 at 10 years and 3 at 13 years). Of the 15 children, 12 (80%) had school achievement problems at age 10 years, and 11 (73%) still had such problems at age 13. This was compared to 8% in the control group and 26% in the situational group at 13 years (Gillberg & Gillberg, 1988).

It should be noted here that the cooccurrence of these other conditions, particularly Conduct Disorder, significantly affects outcome prognosis. More information regarding comorbidity is presented in the concluding chapter of this book.

An earlier population study conducted in a midwestern university town by Werry and Quay (1971) found that in this 5- to 8-year-old population, boys tended to have a higher prevalence rate for acting out or disruptive behavior, while girls showed signs of excess neurotic symptoms. There was a tendency for symptoms in both sexes to decrease between the ages of 5 and 6, with a slight increase again at 8 years. Victor and Halverson (1976) confirmed in their study that the behavior dimensions of Distractibility and Conduct Problem were stable over 2 years for boys and girls selected from a normal population in the early elementary grades. Behavioral problems were also found to be more predictive of later achievement difficulties.

ADAPTIVE FUNCTIONING, SOCIAL SKILLS, AND PARENT INTERACTIONS

ADD is a lifelong disorder that is in most instances pervasive, affecting all aspects of the individual's life. While some children and adults have attentional deficits that are situationally specific, causing problems only at school or the workplace, the majority of individuals with ADD exhibit symptoms that affect all aspects of their lives, including peer and family relationships. Marcel Kinsbourne addresses these issues and their implications for treatment in an article entitled, "Quality of Life in Children with ADHD." In this article he states that "ADHD management should constitute a prime example of treatment targeted on quality-of-life considerations" (Kinsbourne, 1992, p. 1). He writes that there is an undue emphasis in this country on the impact of ADHD on classroom conduct and achievement and that this particular emphasis has far-reaching implications leading to undertreatment and a very shortsighted use of stimulant medication. Kinsbourne asserts that when medication is limited to school hours and home-work, treatment does not address the child's needs for more comprehensive coverage (Kinsbourne, 1992).

Confirmation of significant social and adaptive dysfunc-tion in children with ADD has recently been documented by researchers using the Vineland Social Adaptive Scale (Vine-land). While this instrument has long been used in children with developmental disabilities, its use has not been under-taken routinely as part of the standard evaluation of children with ADD. The Vineland, however, has the potential of being a useful tool not only during the evaluation process but also as a measure of the effectiveness of various intervention/treat-ment strategies.

Recent reports of studies using the Vineland (Barkley, 1990) confirmed that the effects of ADD in childhood seemed to be pervasive, causing problems in all areas of adaptive function-ing across a variety of situations. A rather extensive study evaluating adaptive functioning in children with ADD was more recently carried out by Roizen and colleagues at the University of Chicago (1994). In this study, 104 children who met the criteria for a diagnosis of ADD based on DSM-III-R were evaluated using the Vineland Social Adaptive Scale and the WISC-R intelligence tests. Results indicated that despite the fact that children's mean IQ scores were in the average range (101+/-16), their Vineland scores were in the border-line to low-average range and 27.9 points lower than their IQ scores (almost 2 standard deviations). Further, it was noted that children with ADD and comorbid disorders (disruptive behavior disorder or a learning disability) had significantly lower scores on all three factor domains and socialization scores on the Vineland than children with ADD alone. Data also revealed a significant increase in the discrepancy between IQ scores and Vineland scores as ADD children grew older. In addition, the higher the IQ score, the greater the discrepancy between the IQ and Vineland.

The comment by the authors of this study—that these pre-

liminary findings may have important diagnos
therapeutic implications—seems valid. These
indicate that deficits in adaptive behavior, or
the demands of daily living, may be an import.
tic feature of ADD in children. Their further s|
whether the treatment of adaptive dysfunct:
prove the symptoms and outcomes of children
deserves consideration (Roizen et al., 1994).

Restlessness or overactivity, poor impulse control, inatten-
tiveness to details and instruction, constant talking or inter-
rupting during conversations, changing the rules while playing, and lack of task completion and follow-through are all
typical behaviors of children with ADD which affect day-to-day
functioning. Certainly many of these characteristics cause them
to be in conflict with their social environment and are reflected in the quality of both peer and parent relationships.

Early studies in this area by Campbell (1973) found that
mothers of hyperactive children tended to give their children
considerably more help and encouragement during difficult
tasks than did the mothers of impulsive or reflective children.
Similar findings were made when the interactions of the hyperactive, learning disabled, and normal boys with their mothers were compared. In this study (Campbell, 1975), the hyperactive children were found to be less compliant and the
mothers more directive and encouraging.

Barkley and colleagues have done numerous studies looking at the characteristic of mother–child interactions and the
effects of stimulant medications on this relationship. In the
first study in this area, Cunningham and Barkley (1979) observed 20 normal and 20 hyperactive boys ranging in age from
6 to 12 years as they interacted with their mothers during a
15-minute free play and a 15-minute structured task. These
observations confirmed that hyperactive boys were more active, less compliant, and less likely to remain on task than the
normal controls. The mothers of these hyperactive boys gave
significantly more commands and were less likely to respond

positively to the child's attempts at social interactions during free play situations.

A similar pattern of diminished responsiveness was seen in the hyperactive boys' reaction to their mothers. Noting that mothers imposed more structure and control on the child's play, social interactions, and task-oriented activities, the investigators questioned whether this controlling, intrusive style —which initially may have been a response to the child's behaviors—might further contribute to the child's behavioral difficulties.

Findings in this and other studies were independent of age, but boys in general, whether hyperactive or "normal," were found to be more compliant as they got older. Mothers also tended to give fewer commands and were less controlling over time. While the interactions of hyperactive boys seemed to improve as they got older, they continued to have more behavioral difficulties than their peers in social situations that required increasing demands. (Barkley, Karlsson, & Pollard, 1985).

Sex differences were found to affect the mother–child relationship as well, with hyperactive boys receiving more direction and praise than hyperactive girls or normal boys. Mothers of hyperactive boys also tended to initiate fewer interactions than the mothers of hyperactive girls (Befera & Barkley, 1985).

Stimulant medication as a treatment regimen was investigated and found to induce changes in these mother–child interactions. A double-blind drug trial using two doses of Ritalin was carried out on 60 hyperactive mother–child pairs during free play and structured task situations. While no effects were found during the free play situation, several effects were noted during the specific task situations. Higher doses of Ritalin (methylphenidate) improved both compliance and the duration of compliance in the affected children. Both doses of stimulant were found to result in a decrease in mothers' controlling reactions to the child's noncompliant and off-task behavior. Improvement in home ratings were also noted on medication (Barkley, Karlsson, Pollard, & Murphy, 1985).

Barkley (1985) suggests that these studies have certain implications for clinical practice with hyperactive children. Indeed, the assessment of the social interaction between these children and their parents may prove useful in determining the difficulties to be addressed in developing a treatment protocol. These studies also confirm that there is a situational nature to the misbehavior of these children and that finding in itself should not rule out the diagnosis of ADD. Conversely, examining these variations in behaviors as part of the initial assessment of these children may assist clinicians in achieving a better understanding of the child and his or her deficits.

ADD AND LEARNING DISABILITIES

Numerous studies now indicate that children diagnosed with ADD have learning difficulties and are at great risk for academic failure (Cantwell & Saterfield, 1978; Huessy & Cohen, 1976; Lambert & Sandoval, 1980; Anderson et al., 1987). Specific learning disabilities have also been documented. Approximately 50% of children diagnosed with ADD using DSM-III-R criteria were reported to have a specific learning disability (Shaywitz & Shaywitz, 1988) or more specifically a reading disability (Dykman & Ackerman, 1991).

In the latter study addressing reading disabilities, more boys than girls (9:1) were found to meet the criteria for a specific reading disability. Several other significant findings were also reported. Boys with ADD who did *not* have a reading disability were found to have higher IQs than those who did meet criteria for the disability. Both ADD groups, whether with or without a reading disability, could be differentiated from a control group on measures of sustained attention and impulse control. Stimulant medication (Ritalin) in either high or low dosage was noted to benefit all subgroups equally (Dykman & Ackerman, 1991).

While such specific learning disabilities (LD) do occur, many children with ADD are found to have difficulties in performance as a result of deficiencies in planning, organization, and motivation that do not meet criteria for a specific diagnosis of learning disabilities (Joseph, 1987; Pennington, 1991). These children with ADD have features of what is called an "executive function disorder." Characteristics include difficulty in planning, organizing, resisting distractions, and avoiding impulsive responding. Denckla (1989) refers to these functions as the "overlap zone" between ADD and LD.

It is this "blurring of boundaries" between ADD and LD that results in difficulty separating behavioral from cognitive symptoms in children diagnosed with ADD (Epstein et al., 1991). Attentional deficits resulting in poor executive functioning may be even more important than behavioral deficits, as there is now significant evidence to suggest that children with ADD without hyperactivity are at a more significant risk for academic failure than the children with ADD and hyperactivity (Lahey et al., 1987).

But do these children with ADD and academic failure have specific learning disabilities? Experts contend that deficits within the cognitive domain or "executive dysfunction" may instead be the cause of this academic failure in ADD children, not specific learning disabilities (Denckla, 1989). Cantwell and Baker (1991) address this same issue, stating that their own research and other literature reviewed indicates that ADD and LD are associated to a much greater degree than would occur by chance; however, the nature of that association is unclear. They suggest that perhaps there are subtypes of ADD and/or subtypes of LD, and there may be an association between only some of those subtypes. Children with deficits in the components of attention may be one such subgroup.

Identification of behavioral and cognitive subtypes of ADD and the further delineation of the underlying linguistic deficits that present in children with ADD also appeared promising. The investigators concluded by urging that future research concentrate on subtypes of the population with ADD and subtypes of the population with LD (Cantwell & Baker, 1991).

ADD AND SELF-ESTEEM

It seems only logical that children experiencing difficulties in their social environment as well as academic failures would develop poor self-concepts and low self-esteem (Weiss et al., 1978). In a study by Campbell and coworkers (1977), children with ADD were found to already have lower self-esteem by grades 1 and 2. Hyperactive children, ages 6 to 12, may have poor self-esteem, resulting in some being in actual states of clinical depression. (Weiss & Hechtman, 1993, p. 36). In their 15-year follow-up study, hyperactive young adults were found to have more emotional problems, poor self-esteem, and to not be happy with their life situations (Weiss & Hechtman, 1993).

MULTIMODAL TREATMENT PROGRAMS

As children with ADD have multiple difficulties across various domains of functioning, the need to establish a comprehensive treatment protocol is critical. This multimodal program must be family- and school-based and implemented with consistency in order to strengthen relationships and improve functioning. The four main areas that need to be addressed are as follows:

Education About ADD: This should involve the child, parents, and significant others and deal with the symptoms, diagnosis, etiology, treatment, and impact of ADD on the child and his or her environment.

Psychological Support: May involve individual psychotherapy, but behavior management and self-esteem enhancement programs are critical. Cognitive therapies may be used once the child is mature enough to handle the concepts involved and biofeedback may be useful, especially for relaxation.

Academic Support: Educational interventions should include classroom accommodations as needed, tutoring, and/or special education services to address any documented learning disabilities. Other related services such as occupational, physical, and language therapies should be prescribed as needed.

Medication: Use of medication to address symptoms of ADD and any comorbid conditions remains a fundamental component of appropriate treatment. Other health issues such as asthma or allergies and mental health disorders that are known to be responsive to pharmacologic intervention also need treatment to ensure a successful outcome.

ALL ABOUT EDUCATION

In addition to meeting with a caring and knowledgeable professional, I find that bibliotherapy can be a very powerful tool in assisting the child with ADD and his or her family in their understanding of the disorder. Today, there are literally hundreds of books and several excellent videos available that address the topic of ADD. Only a few are mentioned here. In no way does this constitute an endorsement of any particular book or product, and several excellent resources may have been omitted due to space constraints.

Resources for Parents

Maybe You Know My Kid: A Parent's Guide to Identifying, Understanding, and Helping Your Child with Attention Defi-

cit Hyperactivity Disorder by Mary Fowler, 1990, New York: Birch Lane Press. 239 pages, $12.95.

Taking Charge of ADHD: The Complete Authoritative Guide for Parents by Russell Barkley, 1995, New York: Guilford Press. 294 pages, $16.95.

All About Attention Deficit Disorder: The Information, Tools, and Emotional Support You Need, Video and book by Thomas Phelan, Glen Ellyn, IL: Child Management. (800-442-4453), 165 pages.

Attention Deficit Disorder and Learning Disabilities: Realities, Myths, and Controversial Treatments by Barbara Ingersoll and Sam Goldstein, 1993, New York: Doubleday. 240 pages, $12.95.

Your Hyperactive Child: A Parent's Guide to Coping with Attention Deficit Disorder by Barbara Ingersoll, 1988, New York: Doubleday. (800-223-6834), 219 pages, $9.95.

ADD: Helping Your Child: Untying the Knot of Attention Deficit Disorders by Warren Umansky and Barbara Smalley, 1994, New York: Warner Books. (800-759-0190), 210 pages, $10.99.

More Everyday Parenting: The Six- to Nine-Year-Old by Robin Goldstein and Janet Gallant, 1991, New York: Penguin Books. (800-331-4624), 224 pages, $9.95.

Dr. Larry Silver's Advice to Parents on Attention-Deficit Hyperactivity Disorder by Larry Silver, 1993, Washington DC: American Psychiatric Press. 260 pages, $20.00.

The Parent's Guide to Attention Deficit Disorder by Stephen McCarney and Angela Bauer, 1990, Columbia, MO: Hawthorne Educational Services. 160 pages, $13.00.

Resources for Children

So often the child is left out of the instruction loop. It is vitally important that patients themselves have an understanding of both their ADD and the rationales behind treatment in order to be more active participants in the process.

Putting on the Brakes: Young People's Guide to Understanding Attention Deficit Hyperactivity Disorder by Patricia Quinn and Judith Stern, 1991, New York: Magination Press. (800-825-3089), 64 pages, $9.95.

Putting on the Brakes Activity Book by Patricia Quinn and Judith Stern, 1993, New York: Magination Press. 88 pages, $14.95.

Learning to Slow Down and Pay Attention by Kathleen Nadeau and Ellen Dixon, 1993, Annandale, VA: Chesapeake Psychological Publications. 70 pages, $9.95.

Otto Learns About His Medicine, Revised Edition by Michael Gavin, 1995, New York: Magination Press. 32 pages, $11.95.

Distant Drums, Different Drummers by Barbara Ingersoll, 1995, Bethesda, MD: Cape Publications. 42 pages, $15.95.

Eagle Eyes: A Child's View of Attention Deficit Disorder by Jeanne Gehret, 1991, Fairport, NY: Verbal Images Press. (716-377-8707), 32 pages, $9.95.

Resources for Professionals

Attention-Deficit Hyperactivity Disorder: Handbook for Diagnosis and Treatment by Russell Barkley, 1990, New York: Guiford Publications. (800-365-7006), 747 pages, $50.00.

Attention-Deficit Hyperactivity Disorder: A Clinical Workbook by Russell Barkley, 1991, New York: Guilford Publications. 112 pages, $25.00.

Managing Attention Deficit Disorders in Children: A Guide for Practitioners by Sam Goldstein and Michael Goldstein, 1990, New York: Wiley. (800-225-5945), 451 pages, $52.00.

The Attending Physician: An ADD Guide for Pediatricians by Stephen Copps, 1992, Atlanta, GA: SPI Press. 180 pages, $30.00.

PSYCHOLOGICAL SUPPORT

This aspect of the treatment usually involves dealing with the dual facets of the child's behavior and self-esteem. Effective treatment should be geared to address not only the maladaptive behavior but also the fall-out that behavior has created, particularly its cost in lowered self-esteem. Frequently, children with ADD do need a period of individual psychotherapy to deal with both the primary and secondary issues that having ADD has created in their lives.

Behavioral therapy has come to be an integral part of the treatment plan and has been successfully combined with stimulant medication (Pelham et al., 1986). Practitioners often integrate behavior management techniques into more traditional psychotherapy. This includes work with parents and caregivers along with programs to be carried out by teachers in the school setting (Coker & Thyer, 1990). These family- and school-based interventions have proven successful not only in improving behaviors but also in addressing academic success. Coupling a behavior management program with rewards at home for school behavior can be particularly effective. In any behavior management program, immediacy of consequences and consistency over time have come to be the hallmarks of success.

Self-verbalization or cognitive training has also been advocated as a means of dealing with some of the symptoms of ADD. Cognitive training proposes to improve self-concept and address the deficits in self-guiding the language-based behaviors seen in individuals with ADD through modeling, rehearsal, self-instruction, and self-reinforcement. This therapy encompasses both feelings and behaviors and attempts to deal with the lack of self-control and inability to plan ahead seen in children with ADD. The individual is taught to replace negative self-statements with positive ones, thereby improving self-esteem. Outcome studies have been varied and somewhat inconsistent (Whalen et al., 1985).

Combining behavior management and cognitive therapy has not produced better results than either treatment alone. It also appears that positive effects achieved at home do not generalize to the classroom (Horn et al., 1987). This group also performed a double-blind study that involved the combination of medication with parent training and self-control instruction. There was no evidence of additive effects and they found limited support that the combined treatments produced greater maintenance after therapies were withdrawn (Ialongo et al., 1993).

Cognitive behavioral progress can be effective in children with ADD for improving social skills as well as modifying behaviors. Several steps are usually involved in this process. They include defining the behavior causing the problem that the child would like to change. Modeling and role-playing can then be used as powerful tools to teach new behavioral strategies. These techniques can further be used to allow the child to explore alternative solutions, decide on a plan of action, and practice planning ahead. Many health professionals conduct social skills groups where the child can learn and practice these individual skills in a group setting.

Resources for Parents

BEHAVIOR MANAGEMENT

1-2-3 Magic: Training Your Children To Do What You Want!, 2nd Edition by Thomas Phalen, 1995, Glen Ellyn: IL: Child Management. (800-442-4453), 192 pages, $10.00. Also available as a video (including book) $39.95.

Good Behavior by Stephen Garber, Marianne D. Garber, and Robyn F. Spizman, 1987, New York: Random House. 476 pages, $22.50.

COGNITIVE THERAPY/SOCIAL SKILLS

I Think I Can, I Know I Can: Using Self-Talk to Help Raise Confident, Secure Kids by Susan Isaacs and Wendy Ritchey, 1991, New York: St. Martins. $3.95.

Feelings About Friends by Linda Schwartz, 1988, Santa Barbara, CA: The Learning Works. (800-235-5767), 32 pages, $4.95.

"Wanna Be My Friends?": How to Strengthen Your Child's Social Skills by Leanne Donash and Judith Sachs, 1994, New York: Hearst Books. (800-843-9389), $12.00.

SELF-ESTEEM

101 Ways to Make Your Child Feel Special by Vicki Lansky, 1991, Chicago, IL: Contemporary Books. (312-540-4500), 114 pages, $6.95.

The Winning Family: Increasing Self-Esteem in Your Children and Yourself by Louise Hart, 1993, Berkeley, CA: Celestial Arts. (800-841-2665), 264 pages, $12.95.

Self-Esteem: A Family Affair by Jean Illsley Clarke, 1985, San Francisco: HarperCollins. (800-331-3761), 180 pages, $12.95.

Resources for Teachers and Clinicians

BEHAVIOR MANAGEMENT

Pediatric Compliance: A Guide for the Primary Care Physician by Edward Christopherson, 1994, New York: Plenum Medical Books. 475 pages, $55.00.

Therapies for Children: A Handbook of Effective Treatments for Problem Behaviors by Charles Schaefer and Howard Millman, San Francisco: Jossey-Bass.

Advances in Therapies for Children by Charles Schaefer and Howard Millman, et al. San Fransico: Jossey-Bass. A companion volume to the one described above.

COGNITIVE STRATEGIES/SOCIAL SKILLS

Cognitive-Behavorial Therapy with ADHD Children: Child, Family, and School Interventions by Lauren Braswell and Michael Bloomquist, 1991, New York: Guilford Press. 391 pages, $40.00.

Cognitive-Behavioral Therapy for Impulsive Children, 2nd Edition by Philip Kendall and Lauren Braswell, 1993, New York: Guilford Press. 239 pages, $27.95.

I Can Problem Solve: An Interpersonal Cognitive Problem-Solving Program for Children by Myrna Shure, 1992, Champaign, IL: Research Press.

Think Aloud: Increasing Social and Cognitive Skills—A Problem Solving Program for Children by Bonnie Camp and Mary Ann Bash, 1981, Champaign, IL: Research Press. 296 pages, $49.95.

SELF-ESTEEM

Self-Esteem: A Classroom Affair, Volumes I and II by Michelle and Craig Borba, 1978 (Vol. I), 1982 (Vol. II), San Francisco: HarperCollins. (800-331-3761), 144 pages each, $14.00 each.

Marvelous Me by Linda Schwartz, 1979, Santa Barbara, CA: The Learning Works. (800-235-5767), 32 pages, $3.95.

A catalogue of material geared to improving self-esteem is also available from the Self-Esteem Shop at 4607 N. Woodward, Royal Oak, MI 48073 or by calling 800-251-8336.

Resources for Children

SELF-ESTEEM

Just Because I Am: A Child's Book of Affirmations by Lauren Murphy Paine, 1994, Minneapolis, MN: Free Spirit Publishers. (800-735-7323, 32 pages, $6.95. A very useful Leader's Guide ($12.95) is also available from the publisher.

What Do You Think?: A Kid's Guide to Dealing with Daily Dilemmas by Linda Schwartz, 1993, Santa Barbara, CA: The Learning Works. 184 pages, $ 9.95.

What Would You Do?: A Kid's Guide to Tricky and Sticky Situations by Linda Schwartz, 1990, Santa Barbara, CA: The Learning Works. 184 pages, $9.95.

ACADEMIC SUPPORT

Although the vast majority of children with ADD will have learning difficulties that impair academic performance, not all will require special education services to address these needs. Approximately 45 to 50% of children with ADD do not manifest educational impairments that require special education services; they remain in a regular classroom for their education. Modifications or adaptations within the regular classroom are expected to be sufficient for these children. Another group of children, about 35 to 40% of all diagnosed cases of ADD, are expected to need special education services. Reports indicate that these services can be delivered in a regular classroom setting. However, about 10 to 15% of children with ADD will have academic impairments sufficient to warrant delivery of special education services within a self-contained classroom (Swanson et al., 1992).

Within the regular classroom, teachers must become aware of the needs of the children they serve. This includes education regarding ADD, its symptoms, and impact of ADD on the child, both in the classroom, with peers, and at home, with his or her family. Teachers need to provide structure yet be adaptable and caring. They need the support of the administration, other faculty, and school psychologists to effectively deal with the behaviors related to ADD as they appear in the classroom. Teachers must be taught the basic principles and techniques of behavior management and should work closely with the school nurse and psychologist.

Classroom accommodations can be very effective in helping the child with ADD to successfully achieve academically. A 504 Accommodation Plan (see Chapter 9) allows all involved to develop strategies to deal with each child's unique needs and design an individualized program that specifically addresses these needs. These accommodations are usually very simple and do not tend to be very costly. In addition to providing a structured learning environment, they include providing preferential seating in the classroom, allowing the hyperactive child more freedom to move around the classroom or the building, tailoring homework and class assignments, modifying test delivery, simplifying verbal instructions, using more visual aids, and setting up a modification system that reinforces positive behavior.

There are now several books and programs available to help educators deal more effectively with the child with ADD in the classroom. They include the following:

RESOURCES FOR EDUCATORS

How to Reach and Teach ADD/ADHD Children by Sandra Reif, 1993, New York: Simon & Schuster. 240 pages, $28.00.

The ADD Hyperactivity Handbook for Schools by Harvey Parker, 1992, Plantation, FL: Specialty Press. Available from the A.D.D. Warehouse (800-233-9273), 330 pages, $27.00 paperback, $36.00 hardback.

ADAPT: Attention Deficit Accommodation Plan for Teaching by Harvey Parker. Available from A.D.D. Warehouse. (800-233-9273). This includes a plan book for teachers and one for students and provides strategies to help with problems of inattention, overactivity, disorganization, and impulsivity. The kit is $22.00.

Teaching Students with Attention Deficit Disorders: A Slide Program for In-Service Teacher Training by Harvey Parker and Michael Gordon. Available from A.D.D. Warehouse. (800-233-9273), $150.00.

Structuring Your Classroom for Academic Success by Stan Paine, JoAnn Radicchi, Lynne Rosellini, Leslie Deutchman, and Craig Darch, 1993, Champaign, IL: Research Press. 188 pages, $16.00

A Teacher's Guide: Attention Deficit Disorder in Children, 3rd Edition by Sam Goldstein and Michael Goldstein, 1995, Salt Lake City, UT: Neurology, Learning, and Behavior Center. (801-532-1484), 20 pages, $4.00.

An excellent book for mental health professionals as well teachers is *School-Based Assessment and Interventions for ADD Students* by James Swanson. This manual covers the basic techniques and principles of behavior modification, social skills training, and cognitive therapy as they apply to ADD children in a regular education setting. 184 pages, $22.00.

Attention Deficit Disorder: Strategies for School-Age Children by Clare Jones, 1994, San Antonio, TX: The Psychological Corporation. 211 pages, $39.00.

A resource for parents as well as teachers is the book:
Negotiating the Special Education Maze: A Guide for Parents and Teachers, 2nd Edition by Winifred Anderson, Stephen Chitwood, and Deidre Hayden, 1990, Bethesda, MD: Woodbine House. 269 pages, $14.95.

MEDICATION

Psychopharmacologic treatment of ADD continues to be the mainstay of any intervention program. Their high efficacy rate in dealing with the symptoms and behaviors associated with the disorder have made psychostimulants the first line of treatment. They should, however, not be considered "the only answer," as other intervention strategies—including behavior management and cognitive therapies—have proven to be effective as well.

Medication for ADD, its efficiency and side effects, is the focus of Chapter 8 of this book. All aspects of medication use including psychopharmacologic treatment of comorbid conditions and combined drugs will be discussed further there.

CONCLUSION

More than 50% of the children with ADD are diagnosed by the elementary school years. Many others are diagnosed during this period, as the stresses and structure of the classroom and with peer relationships increase. ADD is a very complex disorder that creates needs across several domains; a comprehensive treatment program is essential to help these children and their families cope. The purpose of this treatment should always be to improve the quality of life of the child and his or her family—not just to address issues related to school and academic achievement. Early intervention is critical, and a coordinated program between home and school is essential to success.

REFERENCES

American Psychiatric Association. (1994). *Diagnostic and statistical manual of mental disorders* (4th ed.). Washington, DC: Author.

Anderson, J. C., Williams, S., McGee, R., & Silva, P. A. (1987). DSM-III disorders in preadolescent children. *Archives of General Psychiatry, 44,* 69–76.

Barkley, R. A. (1985). The social behavior of hyperactive children: Developmental changes, drug effects, and situational variation.

In R. McMahon (Ed.), *Childhood disorders* (pp. 218–243). New York: Brunner/Mazel.

Barkley, R. A. (1990). Nature and diagnosis. In R. A. Barkley (Ed.), *Attention deficit hyperactivity disorder: A handbook for diagnosis and treatment* (pp. 3–38). New York: Guilford Press.

Barkley, R. A., Karlsson, J., & Pollard, S. (1985). Effects of age on the mother–child interactions of ADD-H and normal boys. *Journal of Abnormal Child Psychology, 13*, 631–637.

Barkley, R. A., Karlsson, J., Pollard, S., & Murphy, J. V. (1985). Developmental changes in the mother–child interactions of hyperactive boys: Effects of two dose levels of Ritalin. *Journal of Child Psychology and Psychiatry, 26*, 705–715.

Befera, M. S., & Barkley, R. A. (1985). Hyperactive and normal girls and boys: Mother–child interaction, parent psychiatric status and child psychopathology. *Journal of Child Psychology and Psychiatry, 26*, 439–452.

Blondis, T. A., Accardo, P. J., & Snow, J. H. (1989). Measures of attention, Part I: Questionnaires. *Clinical Pediatrics, 28*, 222–228.

Campbell, S. B. (1973). Mother–child interaction in reflective, impulsive, and hyperactive children. *Developmental Psychology, 8*, 341–349.

Campbell, S. B. (1975). Mother–child interaction: A comparison of hyperactive, learning disabled, and normal boys. *American Journal of Orthopsychiatry, 45*, 51–57.

Campbell, S., Schleifer, M., Weiss, G., & Periman, T. (1977). A two-year follow-up of hyperactive preschoolers. *American Journal of Orthopsychiatry, 47*, 149–162.

Cantwell, D. P., & Baker, L. (1989). Stability and natural history of *DSM-III* childhood diagnoses. *Journal of the American Academy of Child and Adolescent Psychiatry, 28*, 691–700.

Cantwell, D. P., & Saterfield, J. H. (1978). Prevalence of academic achievement in hyperactive children. *Journal of Pediatric Psychology, 3*, 168–171.

Coker, K. H., & Thyer, B. A. (1990). School- and family-based treatment of children with attention-deficit hyperactivity disorder. *Families in Society: Journal of Contemporary Human Services, May*, 276–282.

Cunningham, C. E., & Barkley, R. A. (1979). The interactions of hyperactive and normal children with their mothers in free play and structured tasks. *Child Development, 50,* 217–224.

Denckla, M. B. (1989). Executive function: The overlap zone between attention deficit hyperactivity disorder and learning disabilities. *International Pediatrics, 4,* 155–160.

Dykman, R. A., & Ackerman, P. T. (1991). Attention deficit disorder and specific reading disability: Separate but often overlapping disorders. *Journal of Learning Disabilities, 24,* 96–103.

Epstein, M. A., Shaywitz, S. E., Shaywitz, B. A., & Woolston, J. L. (1991). The boundaries of attention deficit disorder. *Journal of Learning Disabilities, 24,* 78–86.

Gillberg, C., & Gillberg, C. (1988). Generalized hyperkinesis: Follow-up study from age 7 to 13 years. *Journal of the American Academy of Child and Adolescent Psychiatry, 27,* 55–59.

Horn, W., Ialongo, N., Popovich, S., & Peradotto, D. (1987). Behavioral parent training and cognitive-behavioral self-control therapy with ADHD children: Comparative and combined effects. *Journal of Clinical Child Psychology, 16,* 57–68.

Huessy, H. R., & Cohen, A. H. (1976). Hyperkinetic behaviors and learning disabilities followed over seven years. *Pediatrics, 57,* 4–10.

Ialongo, N. S., Horn, W. F., Pascoe, J. M., et al. (1993). The effects of multimodal intervention with attention-deficit hyperactivity disorder children: A 9-month follow-up. *Journal of the American Academy of Child and Adolescent Psychiatry, 32,* 182–189.

Joseph, J. (1987). Learning disabilities due to primary deficiency of planning, organization, and motivation. *Neurology, 37* (Supplement), 221.

Kinsbourne, M. (1992). Quality of life in children with ADHD. *Challenge, 6,* 1–2.

Lahey, B. B., Schaughency, E. A., Hynd, G. W., Carlson, C. L., & Nieves, N. (1987). Attention deficit disorder with and without hyperactivity: Comparison of behavioral characteristics of clinic-referred children. *Journal of the American Academy of Child and Adolescent Psychiatry, 26,* 718–723.

Lambert, N. M., & Sandoval, J. (1980). The prevalence of learning disabilities in a sample of children considered hyperactive. *Journal of Abnormal Child Psychology, 8,* 33–50.

Pelham, W., Walker, J., & Milich, R. (1986). Effects of continuous and partial reinforcement and methylphenidate on learning in children with attention deficit disorder. *Journal of Abnormal Psychology, 95*, 319–325.

Pennington, B. F. (1991). *Diagnosing learning disorders: A neuropsychological framework.* New York: Guilford Press.

Roizen, N. J., Blondis, T. A., Irwin, M., & Stein, M. (1994). Adaptive functioning in children with attention-deficit hyperactivity disorder. *Archives of Pediatric and Adolescent Medicine, 148,* 1137–1142.

Sharp, N. (1993). *Comparing the technical aspects of attention deficit disorders rating scales.* Columbia, MO: Hawthorne Educational Services.

Shaywitz, S. E., & Shaywitz, B. (1988). Attention deficit disorder: Current perspectives. In J. F. Kavanagh & T. J. Truss (Eds.), *Learning disabilities: Proceedings of the national conference* (pp. 369–523). Parkton, MD: York Press.

Swanson, J. M., Kotkin, R., Pfiffer, L., & McBurnett, K. (1992). School-based interventions for ADD students. *Chadder, 6,* 8–9, 22.

Victor, J. B., & Halverson, C. F. (1976). Behavior problems in elementary school children: A follow-up study. *Journal of Abnormal Child Psychology, 4*(1), 17–29.

Weiss, G., & Hechtman, L. T. (1993). *Hyperactive children grown up* (2nd ed.). New York: Guilford Press.

Weiss, G., Hechtman, L., & Perlman, T. (1978). Hyperactive as young adults: School, employers, and self-rating scales obtained during ten-year follow-up evaluation. *American Journal of Orthopsychiatry, 48,* 438–445.

Werry, J. S., & Quay, H. C. (1971). The prevalence of behavior symptoms in younger elementary school children. *American Journal of Orthopsychiatry, 41,* 136–143.

Whalen, C., Hinker, B., & Hinshaw, S. (1985). Cognitive-behavioral therapies for hyperactive children: Premises, problems, and prospects. *Journal of Abnormal Child Psychology, 13,* 391–410.

Chapter 5

THE ADOLESCENT/
HIGH SCHOOL STUDENT

Although studies indicate that from 15 to 50% of children with ADD ultimately outgrow their problems or are at least no longer affected by the symptoms, most ADD children continue to have difficulty with functioning into young adulthood. The changes and stresses inherent to this developmental period frequently adversely affect the adolescent who may have stabilized during later childhood or cause an undiagnosed individual to seek attention for the first time. The clinician must feel comfortable dealing with this population and recognizing the symptoms of ADD and the other comorbid conditions particular to this age group. Information for this task can be gathered from recent follow-up studies.

FOLLOW-UP STUDIES

In a group of children diagnosed with ADD between 6 and 12 years of age, approximately 50 to 70% continued to manifest troublesome symptoms through middle adolescence (Gittleman et al., 1985). A Swedish follow-up study of nonmedicated ADD adolescents found that attentional dysfunction decreased from 100% at age 7 to only 19% by age 13. However, academic problems were present in approximately 70 to 75% of the group and remained stable across ages, as did psychiatric problems. The most common areas of difficulty in the ADD group were reading problems, 75%; depression/anxiety/panic attacks, 65%; motor difficulties, 40%; and substance abuse, 15% (Gillberg, 1994).

Weiss and coworkers (1971), in their 5-year follow-up of hyperactive children diagnosed initially between the ages of 6 and 13 years, found that whereas restlessness had been the main problem for each child 5 years previously, it was no longer the chief complaint for any individual. Some 30% of the group reported that restlessness was still present but not a severe problem. The hyperactivity scores obtained by rating scales on these adolescents were likewise significantly reduced. Distractibility scores were also reduced, although on direct observation in the classroom students with ADD were still less able to concentrate than normal controls. This distractibility or poor concentration was now the chief complaint in 46% of their sample and referred to by many of the subjects themselves. Problems with peer relationships were reported in 30% of the adolescents, and 25% had acting-out antisocial behaviors.

Problems with academic achievement were seen in 80% of the group; 70% of the sample had repeated at least one grade in school; 35% had repeated two or more grades; 10% were in special classes; and 5% had been expelled from school. Only 20% of this group at follow-up were seen as succeeding academically. Those who were more successful had a higher mean IQ score and were rated as less hyperactive and distractible than others in the group. Adolescents with overt antisocial behaviors were noted to differ from the rest of the group by having significantly higher aggression scores on initial evaluation and having families rated as more pathologic.

ACADEMIC AND SOCIAL DIFFICULTIES

Adolescence is a time of many changes, and the last thing a high school student wants is to feel different from his or her peers. It is a time, therefore, when having ADD can be particularly distressing. However, for the majority of adolescents, their ADD symptoms continue to pose both academic and social problems.

Underachievement in high school is a frequent presenting complaint of adolescents with ADD. As a younger student in a self-contained classroom with one teacher, the ADD child may be able to "hold it all together" and perform adequately with support. However, as the demands and stresses of middle/high school increase, such students are less able to compensate and cope successfully. There are several reasons for the underachievement and lack of success among these students.

When children reach adolescence, it is assumed that they have a large repertoire of previously acquired knowledge that they can call upon with minimal effort. Automaticity of functioning in certain areas is expected. This is not the case for students with ADD, particularly if their ADD has only recently been diagnosed. I usually say that these students present like Swiss cheese and have a knowledge base that is "full of holes." These students may have been in attendance when the material was presented, but they certainly were not paying attention and therefore were unable to retrieve that information when it was needed later. A causal relationship between memory and attentional deficits and certain specific dysfunctions of memory have been found to commonly coexist with attention disorders (Levine, 1989).

This connection between attention and memory certainly

has implications for academic achievement. In order to be successful, students with ADD must be evaluated for patterns of strength and weakness in memory functions and processing abilities. Using this information, specific strategies for improving both attention and memory can be addressed. In some instances, the memory load may have to be lessened and/or accommodations made. Students should be made aware of both their attention and/or memory problems as well as the need to remediate deficits in their knowledge base (to "fill in the holes," so to speak). These aspects of diagnosis and treatment play an important role in reducing frustration and improving academic performance, especially in test situations.

Cognitive fatigue is frequently seen in adolescents with ADD. They may tire easily or tend to lack the persistence for task completion. Sleep disorders are present and may include difficulty falling asleep at night and/or waking in the morning. Disorders of arousal may also manifest as fatigue during the day or yawning when concentration is required for a task. Some students have described feeling that they will fall asleep if they sit too long (Quinn, 1994). These problems with arousal contribute to both the inefficiency of attention seen in class as well as the lack of persistence for completion of assignments, resulting in underachievement and dissatisfaction with performance by students, parents, and teachers.

Coleman and Levine (1988), in their review article, have astutely portrayed the scenario of attentional deficits in adolescence and outlined the academic impact of these deficits in Table 2.

Emotional overreactivity is also seen in adolescents with ADD. Behaviors including denial, temper tantrums, and low frustration tolerance, as well as depression and poor self-esteem are seen for the first time, or increase in severity. Girls with ADD have an increased incidence of mood disorders, peer rejection, and low self-esteem. Boys with ADD tend to be more aggressive or oppositional.

It may be difficult for the clinician to differentiate between

TABLE 2
Academic Impacts of Attention Deficits in Adolescence: Associated Problems and Symptoms

Characteristics	Manifestations
Associated processing problems	May have visual-spatial, temporal-sequential language, or reasoning problems. Discrete compensatory skills may be evident.
Associated memory problems	Divergent memory usually stronger than convergent memory. Difficulty with content-rich subjects, especially those emphasizing cumulative knowledge and skills.
Cognitive fatigue	Tendency to tire in school day, especially with passive listening tasks. Often associated with "sleep arousal imbalance."
Fine motor dysfunction	May result from impulsive and hurried style, poor motor memory, or poor motor planning.
Ineffective self-monitoring	Poor execution of quality control over work. "Careless errors" often noted. Ineffective study skills.
Excessive motivation dependency	Inordinate motivational intensity required to sustain attention to routine tasks.
Disorganization	Affects tasks that require organized, systematic routines (e.g., management of time and materials). Lack of strategies or flexibility may be noted.
Performance inconsistency	Day-to-day or even hour-to-hour variation in learning, behavior, and sometimes mood patterns for no apparent reason.
Impersistence	Poor on-task performance in both quality and quantity. Difficulty finishing assignments.
Poor selective attention	Difficulty in distinguishing the salient detail from irrelevant or trivial. Distractibility is major concern.
Abhorrence of or inattention to detail	Tendency to be cursory or superficial. May be good generalizers or conceptual thinkers.

Source: Coleman, W., & Levine, M. (1988). Attention Deficits in Adolescence: Description, Evaluation, and Management. *Pediatrics in Review, 9*(9), 288.

the symptoms of a mood disorder and ADD in the adolescent. Usually, however, the symptoms of ADD have been present for some time, and it is only with adolescence that these other behavioral symptoms appear and are superimposed on the ADD.

ADOLESCENTS WITH PERSISTENT HYPERACTIVITY, AGGRESSIVITY, AND/OR CONDUCT DISORDER

While the symptoms of hyperactivity/impulsivity decrease in many adolescents with ADD, it appears that persistence of these symptoms combined with the additional diagnosis of Conduct Disorder predisposes to a poorer outcome. Impulsivity is found to impair the young adult's ability to make decisions or to stick to a course of action. The adolescent has problems following rules, delaying gratification, and working for larger rewards. He or she may find it difficult to inhibit behaviors as the situation demands or to keep from acting out. Approximately 75% of hyperactive adolescents also have behavioral problems. These include antisocial behavior (25%) and conduct disorder (50%) (Klein & Mannuzza, 1991). An 8-year follow-up study conducted by Barkley and colleagues (1990) found that 80% of the children with ADD were still hyperactive as adolescents and that 60% of them had developed Oppositional Defiant Disorder or Conduct Disorder (Barkley et al., 1990). It appears from the data of numerous studies that continued hyperactivity and impulsivity combined with a diagnosis of Conduct Disorder predicts a poorer outcome. This group of adolescents is at greater risk for more antisocial behavior, substance abuse, and arrests. (Klein & Mannuzza, 1991; Farrington et al., 1989) These adolescents also appear to be involved in more dangerous behaviors as well as an increased incidence of motor vehicle accidents (Weiss & Hechtman, 1993).

However, it now appears that the role of hyperactive and aggressive symptoms may be more complex than previously thought in predicting adolescent outcome. This area has been thoroughly investigated by Loney and colleagues. Their work appears to indicate that aggressivity is in itself a separate entity and stems from a different source than the attentional deficits. This symptom, however, when present, is thought to complicate the problem and worsen the prognosis. From these studies, it is felt that aggression may be more significant than hyperactivity in determining the adolescent outcome of hyperactive children. (Loney et al., 1978; Milich & Loney, 1979).

DIAGNOSIS OF ADD IN THE ADOLESCENT

How can one diagnose ADD in adolescence when so many of these behaviors—inattention, distractibility, and mood swings—are commonly seen during this developmental period? Again, the answer appears to be a matter of degree. A careful history obtained both from the adolescent and the parents is critical. Interviews should be conducted together and individually to allow for independent reporting of symptoms. DSM-IV criteria can be applied to this age group, although some symptoms may not be as prominent.

Chris is 17 years and 10 months old, an eleventh-grade student from a private school that he has attended since kindergarten. While he is generally perceived as a bright adolescent, Chris has struggled academically over the last several years. He reportedly has often found it difficult to follow through and has been on the brink of not being invited back to the school several times.

Recently Chris became impressed by the similarities between his own behavior and school performance and that of a friend with ADHD. He shared this impression with his therapist, a psychiatrist who had treated Chris for depression intermittently over the past two years. This clinician confirmed the diagnosis of ADHD and prescribed Ritalin. Chris reported that he was able to sit and work in a focused manner for five consecutive hours with his first dose of Ritalin, and he demonstrated a dramatic increase in productivity after he began taking medication.

Chris continued to report a very slow reading speed and efficiency, which was suspected to be due to a learning disability. He underwent a complete neuropsychological evaluation, which revealed a marked unevenness in his pattern of abilities. While his verbal IQ score was at the 97th percentile, listening comprehension performance was at the 41st percentile for age, reflecting weak auditory processing skills. Inefficiency in verbal retrieval was noted and a mild learning disability in the area of written language was confirmed.

On the Test of Variables of Attention (TOVA), which is a long and demanding computerized test of attention, Chris made a high number of omission errors (signaling inattention) and a high number of commission errors (indicating impulsivity); his response speed was seen as highly inconsistent. These results were indicative of the inattention, impulsivity, and inconsistency of performance that are hallmarks of ADD.

But why did it take until the eleventh grade to diagnose Chris? If we take some time and review his school records we will see that the symptoms have been there, unrecognized for years. The following are direct quotes obtained from his school files:

Kindergarten teachers reported that Chris "often seemed overwhelmed or bewildered by the many events of the school day. We have felt that his confusion has been caused by inattention during group times." It was also reported that he exhibited difficulty following directions, at times was vague and frequently daydreamed. It was recommended that Chris repeat kindergarten. During this second year teachers continued to be concerned, but when working in a one-to-one situation with extra help with directions, Chris was more successful.

During the first grade teachers were "very pleased with Chris's progress but concerned with his learning style and ability to function independently in the classroom. Chris's attention span is slowly maturing. However it remains very difficult for Chris to focus, follow two- or three-step verbal directions, and complete classroom academic work. He requires much teacher support, feedback, and direction to learn and has worked best in one-to-one instructional settings."

Second grade sounded a similar theme. "He needs much teacher support to get settled, to get started, and to complete a task. He often appears preoccupied with his own thoughts or pursuing his social agenda with friends. Although improved at times, he remains overly dependent on teacher support." After second grade, Chris was placed in a second and third grade combination class, effectively repeating second grade curriculum. Reports indicate that this allowed him "the opportunity to develop some solid academic skills at his own comfortable pace."

In fourth grade, "major difficulties continue to be following oral and written directions, organizing and structuring his assignments and thinking in the abstract." In fifth grade a positive note was finally sounded: "In my four years of working with this age group, Chris has the most outstanding skills in observation and drawing that I have ever seen." Sixth and seventh grade continued the themes of poor attention and concentration. In eighth grade, a referral was made for an academic evaluation, which revealed difficulty in perceptual areas and weak reading and writing skills.

By ninth grade, Chris's difficulties had taken their toll

emotionally and Chris had his first classic major depressive episode. "His thinking about harming himself comes mostly in periods of intense frustration and anger...." Chris's high school career proceeded to be mediocre, with infrequent class participation. One of his teachers summarized his performance in the following words, "Chris sometimes seems to me to be two different people; there is Chris, the hard worker, the one who applied himself at the end of the semester and earned a high B+ on the final exam; and then there is Chris, the half-hearted, fun-loving, at times disruptive, somehow unconnected and underachieving."

The second profile is of a female student who presented in junior high with symptoms of ADD, predominantly inattentive type, and mild learning disabilities.

Emily is a tenth-grade student who performed exceptionally well in elementary school and did not begin to have difficulty until junior high school, when her grades began to deteriorate. Records confirm that by the end of second grade, Emily was reading on a beginning fourth-grade level and advanced in all academic areas. She became frustrated in junior high and complained that she did not understand what she read. She received a full diagnostic evaluation, which revealed both auditory processing and reading comprehension difficulties. Her performance was inconsistent and teacher reports indicated easy distractibility and difficulty concentrating.

Emily was diagnosed as having Attention Deficit Disorder and placed on Ritalin (methylphenidate). Dosage was increased up to 10 mg twice a day without beneficial effect; there were also considerable side effects of nausea, dizziness, and loss of appetite. Cylert (pemoline) was also tried without success. At that time Emily was placed on carefully controlled doses of Dexedrine (dextroamphetamine), which proved extremely effective.

Achievement significantly improved with the combination of stimulant medication, tutoring, and special academic accommodations.

Approximately two years later, Emily became somewhat depressed, although she continued to do well academically. At that time Prozac (fluoxetine) was added to the Dexedrine with a good clinical response. To date, she continues to do well.

RATING SCALES

Standardized rating scales continue to be useful in determining symptomatology. However, in this age group, in addition to teacher and parent rating scales, self-report questionnaires can also be obtained from the adolescent. These scales may be used to facilitate discussions with the adolescent and help him or her quantify some very subjective feelings.

At present there are several rating scales that are useful in the screening of adolescents and older children for ADD. These include the ANSER System Forms (Levine, 1985), the Brown Attention-Deficit Disorder Scale (BADDS) (Brown, 1993), and the ADD/H Adolescent Self-Report Scale (ADD/HSRS) (Conners & Wells, 1985). Each is described briefly here.

The ADD/HSRS consists of 112 items rated by the adolescent on a four-point scale and takes about 10 minutes to complete. The scale is organized into categories that include assets as well as problems with concentration, restlessness, self-control, anger, friends, confidence, learning, feelings, and family. The Conners' *Parent and Teacher Rating Scales* can also be used in conjunction with self-report in this age group to gather more information about performance at home and school. These are designed on a four-point scale for rating behaviors. Both the parent and teacher rating scales have long and short versions and were originally designed and have been used for over 20 years for the identification of hyperactive children. Norms are available for children aged 3 to 17 years.

The Brown ADD Diagnostic Form for Adolescents is a 40-item self-report/parent-report instrument designed by Brown to assess older children and adolescents, 12 to 18 years old, for an attention deficit disorder that does not include hyperactivity. Items are divided into five core clusters of symptoms that include (1) activating and organizing to work, (2) sustaining attention, (3) sustaining energy and effort, (4) mood and rejection sensitivity, and (5) memory recall. This instrument also uses a four-point scale for responses by the adolescent and takes about 10 minutes to administer. Arthur Robin, in his review of rating scales, reports finding this scale particularly useful for adolescents of all ability levels and all varieties of ADHD and offers that both the ADD/HSRS and the BADDS helped "flesh out" the overall clinical picture (Robin, 1994).

The ANSER system is a series of questionnaires to be completed by parents, school personnel, and older children for assessing the development, behavior, and health of children. Form 3 (revised) is designed for secondary school students of ages 12 up. It also contains a Self-Administered Student Profile (Form 4 revised) that allows the adolescent to assess his or her own performance in various areas. Other skills and interests are also inquired about and provide an opportunity for the adolescent to look at personal characteristics and compensatory skills.

There is also a new Adolescent Symptom Inventory-4 (ASI-4) designed by Kenneth Gadow and Joyce Sprafkin as a screening device to assess many of the emotional and behavioral disorders diagnosed in adolescence. This checklist is an extension of the Child Symptom Inventory-4 from the State University of New York at Stony Brook. The ASI-4 is a 122-item checklist that can be completed by parents, teachers, and other care providers who are familiar with the child's problems. It organizes the DSM-IV (1994) diagnoses in a convenient checklist format and facilitates the exchange of information between the parents, school, and clinician.

ADDITIONAL TESTING

Neurodevelopmental and psychoeducational testing should be performed on all adolescents in whom the diagnosis of ADD is being entertained. This will help to determine academic status and degree of neurologic maturation as well as possible learning disabilities. As many as 40% of students with ADD also have coexisting learning disabilities (Barkley, 1990). The presence of these disorders can significantly alter prognosis and affect outcome.

The strengths and weaknesses of the student with ADD must also be carefully delineated. As reported earlier, it should be kept in mind that girls with ADD present somewhat differently and have been found to have more language problems and cognitive deficits. Intelligence testing should be performed. Several studies have now documented improved prognosis with higher intellectual functioning (Brown et al., 1992; 1993).

COMORBID CONDITIONS

The existence of comorbid conditions should be carefully sought out during initial and follow-up interviews. Treatment modalities and choice of psychopharmacologic interventions will ultimately be determined by the presence or absence of other disorders. Adolescents with ADD may show a variety of other disorders including depression, anxiety disorders, panic attacks, obsessive-compulsive disorder, Tourette's syndrome, and conduct disorder in addition to learning disabilities (see Chapter 10 for a further discussion of comorbidity).

The coexistence of any of these conditions will significantly affect choice of treatment modalities; but as ADD is such a complex disorder, all cases will need a multimodal approach.

MULTIMODAL TREATMENT APPROACH

The treatment of ADD in adolescents requires a comprehensive program that addresses all of the young adult's needs. This includes medical, psychological, and behavioral interventions. Special education classes and tutoring may also be needed to ensure academic success. These, combined with classroom adaptations, will make academic challenges easier to cope with for the young adult with ADD. College and vocational counseling can assist in making appropriate placement decisions based on strengths and psychoeducational profile.

MEDICATION

Several trends have been noted over the last several years in respect to use of medication for the treatment of ADD in adolescents, with significantly more elementary students now remaining on stimulant medication for ADD during their high school years. While only 11% of students on medication were in high school in 1975, that number had increased to 30% of all children on medication by 1993. Significant differences were also noted in relation to the use of stimulant treatment in girls, with the gap narrowing from 1:12 females/males being treated in 1981 to a 1:6 female/male ratio of treatment in 1993 (Safer & Krager, 1994).

Several studies have demonstrated the efficacy of stimulant treatment in ADHD in adolescents. In summarizing these studies Wilens & Biederman (1992) go on to point out that the response rate is approximately 75%, with ranges from 70% to 100%. Prior stimulant treatment did not affect outcome, and there was no abuse or tolerance demonstrated in these studies. Increased diastolic blood pressure was seen in black adolescents in one study and increased heart rate was found in another (Wilens & Biederman, 1992).

Stimulant medication is one of the most useful tools in dealing with attentional deficits. However, care must be taken in prescribing medication for this age group in order to assure that the adolescent realizes the importance of compliance with the dosage regimen. Students frequently see the need for medication as confirming that there is something wrong with them and therefore refuse to take their medications or sabotage treatment programs. Acceptance must frequently be one of the issues dealt with in therapy. Counseling regarding caffeine and alcohol ingestion should also take place when stimulants are initially prescribed. Jitteriness and increasing insomnia are usually the result of excess caffeine that students take in colas, coffee, iced tea, and chocolate.

At this stage, the actual consumption of the stimulant medication in the school setting should continue to be supervised. Recreational use of these drugs is again gaining popularity with teens, and the student should not be exposed to the additional pressure of supplying his or her medicine to peers. Supervision also ensures the monitoring of compliance, possible side effects, and efficacy of response by the school nurse or other health room or school personnel.

Catapres (clonidine) may also be effective in this age group to address symptoms of overanxiety, tics, and/or obsessive-compulsive behaviors. When used in combination with the stimulants, it addresses symptoms of overarousal and hyper-vigilance. Sleep disorders frequently respond to a bedtime dose of 0.1 mg.

BEHAVIOR MANAGEMENT AND CONTRACTING

Behavior management programs, commonly used quite successfully for younger children with ADD, are not found to be as effective in the adolescent population (Coleman & Levine, 1988). I personally have found that contracts work much better and can be used to address a specific area of difficulty.

For the problem of missing homework assignments, which commonly contributes to the underachievement of students with ADD, I use a simple contract (see Exhibit 1) for a weekly check that all assignments are completed. This program does carry with it some built-in negative consequences as well as positive rewards, but it can be extremely motivating for the socially active teen or athlete.

For students with disciplinary problems, a contract between the secondary school administration, parents, and the student can be drawn up. This contract should always be signed by all parties involved. Specificity in delineating the rules to be followed and consequences for infractions is critical to the success of this type of program. Students with ADD must have everything spelled out for them in black and white. There should be no room for misinterpretation if this type of contract is to be effective.

Care must be taken to make sure that the student's disabilities are not the basis of the problem. If this is the case, then accommodations may also have to be made to effectively deal with issues.

THERAPY

In working with adolescents with ADD, I have found that they all need some form of supportive counseling. Individual therapy on a short-term basis allows the newly diagnosed student to discuss anger and feelings of frustration. Adolescents with mood disorders need individual psychotherapy to address comorbid conditions and assess the need for additional medications. At this stage, family counseling may be necessary to deal with parent–child conflict effectively and to provide for an exchange of information and ideas on managing

EXHIBIT 1
Weekly Assignment Checksheet

Name: _____   Date: _____

SUBJECT	TEACHER INITIALS	MISSING ASSIGNMENTS

To be initialed each week by all teachers.

Consequences

1. If student forgets sheet—grounded for weekend.
2. Missing assignments must be completed before any contact with friends, TV, phone, etc., Friday P.M. or Saturday A.M. *No exceptions* (even for a sports activity).
3. If all signed as clear and completed—Prearranged *reward* for weekend (pizza, sleepover, movie, later curfew, etc.).

certain behavioral issues. Support groups can be extremely useful in allowing the adolescent to see that he or she is not alone in having this disorder and can provide a forum for sharing effective management strategies and information about ADD.

Skills groups also have proven useful for ADD adolescents. Within this framework, they may address such issues as basic social skills, conversation, and problem-solving skills, including conflict resolution. Here the adolescent can learn to ask for help and work within a group to solve problems.

ACCOMMODATIONS AT THE SECONDARY LEVEL

Students with ADD at the secondary level continue to need an adviser or school counselor to ensure that programs are running smoothly. The student should meet with the adviser on a weekly or daily basis to discuss day-to-day functioning and monitor degree of academic success. This adviser may also assist in setting up a schedule that meets the individual student's needs. Having academic subjects earlier in the day or an additional study period to organize daily work can be invaluable. The need for foreign language waivers or developmental level courses can be determined and subsequently arranged for the student.

In addition, at this stage the student should begin to assume some responsibility for his or her disorder and undertake to become an active self-advocate. This cannot be accomplished overnight, but the student can begin by engaging in the process of developing greater self-awareness with a therapist or counselor. Defining strengths and weaknesses is the first step to designing an individualized program, with specific strategies and accommodations to deal with weaknesses and ensure successful academic performance. The clinician's role at this point is to assist in this self-awareness process through testing, discussion, and training sessions. Metacognitive training to facilitate development of self-knowledge and specific skills such as "how to think and problem solve" has also been found to be useful. Adolescents with ADD need to be taught how to predict the success or failure of a plan of attack and how to modify strategies to ensure success.

Impairments in speed and efficiency of processing information, inattention, retrieval/memory deficits, and motor problems contribute to the academic difficulties seen at the secondary level. Accommodations employing strategies to overcome these difficulties are critical to success. The adolescent must develop a repertoire of strategies that are specific to his unique deficits and gain facility and flexibility in using them to enhance his performance. Developing an individualized 504 Accommodation Plan (see Chapter 9) may facilitate this process; matching a strategy to a specific task demand is, however, critical if the process is to be effective.

Accommodations that are particularly useful at this stage of academic development are listed below. These include modifications to academic requirements and adaptations in both educational programs and curriculum.

Modifications to academic requirements may include:

Untimed and/or oral tests.

Substitution of specific courses needed for completion of degree requirements (usually involves foreign language requirement).

Adaptation in the manner in which specific courses are conducted.

Use of tape recorders/note takers to record lecture classes.

Auxiliary aids such as computers, taped texts, or readers.

Adaptations in education programs may include:

Providing a structured learning environment, including supervised study halls/periods, and tutoring sessions.

Scheduled meetings with an adviser.

Repetition and/or simplification of instructions about in-class and homework assignments.

Supplementing verbal instructions with visual material.

Use of behavior management or contracts.

Adjusting class schedules.

Modifying test delivery.

Use of tape recorders, computers, planners, etc.

Selecting modified textbooks or workbooks.

Providing books on tape.

Tailoring homework assignments.

Individualizing schedule for completion of long-term assignments.

This list is certainly not all-inclusive, and the student and counselor may decide on other accommodations to bolster and improve performance. In addition, the student should be encouraged to meet with individual teachers for clarification of information and informal tutoring on an as-needed basis. This arrangement, in order to be carried out consistently, may have to be formalized and written into the 504 Accommodation Plan.

COLLEGE COUNSELING

With all of the necessary supports, adolescents with ADD can be successful and look forward to continuing their education at the postsecondary level. However, choosing a college for the adolescent with ADD can be one of the most anxiety-provoking situations that parents as well as students have to deal with. The clinician can be useful at this point by making a referral to a qualified placement specialist. In addition, aspects of the student's individualized program that have enabled him or her to be successful should be reviewed. The point of college entrance is not the time to give up these supports, and this may have to be discussed with the student before he or she is caught up in all the changes that accompany a situation of independent living. However, before the student can be considered for admission to the college of his or her choice, the dreaded Scholastic Assessment Tests (SATs) must be taken and usually retaken.

STANDARDIZED TESTING, ESPECIALLY THE SATs

As a result of problems with automaticity of recall, poor time management, perceptual difficulties, disorganization, and dysgraphia (difficulty writing), many students with ADD will have to make arrangements to receive the accommodation of untimed or extended time for testing. This accommodation may have to be applied on a daily basis as well as for standardized testing including the Scholastic Assessment Tests (SATs). Only those students whose schools currently provide them with special accommodations for instruction and assessment are eligible for extended time or other special arrangements on the SATs.

What You Need for Permission to Take the SATs Untimed

The current Educational Testing Service (ETS) requirements for eligibility to take untimed SATs are as follows. A student must have on file at his or her school either a current Individualized Education Program (IEP) or two signed documents, based on test results, obtained during the previous three years from any of the following: physician(s), psychologist(s), child-study team(s), or learning disability specialist(s). Both documents cannot be from the same individual or team.

When a public school normally provides an IEP for a student with a learning disability, that student may not present signed statements in lieu of an IEP in order to obtain extended time and/or other special test arrangements. The IEP must state the nature and effect of the disability and the need for modified testing arrangements. The two signed documents must state and describe the disability, the tests used in diagnosis, and the need for special testing arrangements. In addition, these signed documents must affirm that the disability meets state guidelines for certification when such guidelines exist. The IEP or two signed documents are then retained in the school file unless specifically requested by SAT Services for Students with Disabilities (SAT Program, 1994).

CONCLUSION

Too often ADD has been seen as a disorder of childhood. It is important to realize that many of our young adults can also be affected, sometimes with symptoms first appearing during this period. Difficulties exhibited during childhood do not always disappear, and ADD now appears to be established as a lifelong condition. However, with proper identification, treatment, and support, the young adult can learn to overcome or minimize many of the symptoms and complications of ADD.

RECOMMENDED READINGS

Clinicians may wish to recommend the following books and/ or videos to patients and their families.

BOOKS WRITTEN FOR PARENTS

Surviving Your Adolescents by Thomas Phelan, 1991, Glen Ellyn, IL: Child Management. (800-442-4453), 136 pages, $12.95.

Teenagers with ADD: A Parents' Guide by Chris A. Zeigler Dendy, 1995, Bethesda, MD: Woodbine Press. (800-843-7323), 350 pages, $16.95.

ADHD and Teens: A Parent's Guide to Making It Through the Tough Years by Colleen Alexander-Roberts, 1995, Dallas TX: Taylor. (800-677-2800), 208 pages, $12.95.

BOOKS WRITTEN FOR THE ADOLESCENT

Adolescents and ADD: Gaining the Advantage by Patricia O. Quinn, 1995, New York: Brunner/Mazel. (800-825-3089), 128 pages, $12.95.

Making the Grade: An Adolescent's Struggle with ADD by Roberta Parker, 1992, Plantation, FL: Impact Publications. Available from A.D.D. Warehouse, (800-233-9273), 47 pages, $11.00.

I Would If I Could: A Teenager's Guide to ADHD/Hyperactivity by Michael Gordon, 1992, New York: GSI Publications. (315-446-4849), 34 pages, $12.50.

ADHD: A Teenager's Guide by James Crist, 1996, King of Prussia, PA: The Center for Applied Psychology. (610-277-4020), 176 pages, $27.95.

ADD and the College Student: A Guide for High School and College Students with Attention Deficit Disorder by Patricia O. Quinn (Ed.), 1994, New York: Brunner/Mazel. (800-825-3089), 128 pages, $13.95.

School Strategies for ADD Teens by Kathleen Nadeau, Ellen Dixon, and Susan Biggs, 1993, Annandale, VA: Chesapeake Psychological Publications. (703-642-6697), 46 pages, $7.95.

The Survival Guide for Teenagers with LD by Rhoda Cummings and Gary Fisher, 1993, Minneapolis, MN: Free Spirit Publishing. (800-735-7323), 200 pages, $11.95.

Keeping a Head in School: A Student's Book About Learning Abilities and Learning Disorders by Mel Levine, 1990, Cambridge, MA: Educators Publishing Service. (800-225-5750), 320 pages, $22.00.

FOR THE CLINICIAN

ADHD in Adolescence—The Next Step: A Video Guide for the Clinical Description, Diagnosis, and Treatment of Adolescents with ADHD by Arthur Robin; *Negotiating Parent–Adolescent Conflict: A Behavioral Family Systems Approach* by Arthur Robin and Sharon Foster, 1989, New York: Guilford Press. (800-365-7006), 338 pages, $37.95.

REFERENCES

Barkley, R. A. (1990). Attention deficit hyperactivity disorder: A handbook for diagnosis and treatment. New York: Guilford Press.

Barkley, R. A., Fischer, M., Edelbrock, E. S., & Smallish, L. (1990). The adolescent outcome of hyperactive children diagnosed by research criteria, I: An eight year prospective follow-up study. *Journal of the American Academy of Child and Adolescent Psychiatry, 29,* 546–557.

Brown, T. E. (1993). Attention deficit disorders without hyperactivity. *CHADDER, 7,* 7–10.

Brown, T. E. (1996). Brown attention deficit disorder scales. San Antonio, TX: The Psychological Corporation.

Brown, T. E., & Gammon, C. D. (1993). Attention deficit disorder without hyperactivity in high-IQ adolescents: Assessment instruments and treatment. *Journal of Child and Adolescent Psychopharmacology.*

Brown, T. E., Gammon, C. D., & Barua, G. (1992). Attention-activation disorder in high I.Q. adolescents. Presented at the American Psychiatric Association Conference, Washington, DC.

Coleman, W. L., & Levine, M. D. (1988). Attention deficits in adolescents: Description, evaluation, and management. *Pediatrics in Review, 9*, 287–298.

Conners, C. K., & Wells, K. C. (1985). ADD-H adolescent self-report scale. *Psychopharmacology Bulletin, 21*, 921–922.

Farrington, D. P., Loeber, R., & von Kammen, W. B. (1989). Long-term criminal outcomes of hyperactivity-impulsivity-attention deficit and conduct problems in childhood. In L. N. Robins & M. R. Rutter (Eds.), *Straight and devious pathways to adulthood*. New York: Cambridge University Press.

Gillberg, I. C., & Gillberg C. (1988). Generalized hyperkinesis: Follow-up study from age 7 to 13 years. *Journal of the American Academy of Child and Adolescent Psychiatry, 27*, 55–59.

Gittleman, R., Mannuzza, S., Shenker, S., & Bonagura, N. (1985). Hyperactive boys almost grown up, I: Psychiatric status. *Archives of General Psychiatry, 42*, 937–947.

Hellgren, L., Gillberg, C., & Gillberg, I. C. (1994). Children with deficits in attention, motor control, and perception (DAMP) almost grown up: The contribution of various background factors to outcome at age 16 years. *European Child and Adolescent Psychiatry, 3*, 1–15.

Hellgren, L., Gillberg, I. C., Bagenholm, A., & Gillberg, C. (1994). Children with deficits in attention, motor control, and perception (DAMP) almost grown up: Psychiatric and personality disorders at age 16 years. *Journal of Child Psychology and Psychiatry, 35*(7), 1255–1271.

Klein, R. G., & Mannuzza, S. (1991). Long-term outcome of hyperactive children: A review. *Journal of the American Academy of Child and Adolescent Psychiatry, 30*, 383–387.

Levine, M. D. (1989). Attention and memory: Progression and variation during the elementary school years. *Pediatric Annals, 18*, 366–372.

Levine, M. S. (1985). *The ANSER System*. Cambridge, MA: Educators Publishing Service.

Loney, J., Prinz, R., Mishalow, J., & Joad, J. (1978). Hyperkinetic/aggressive boys in treatment: Predictions of clinical response to methylphenidate. *American Journal of Psychiatry, 135*, 1487–1491.

Milich, R., & Loney, J. (1979). The role of hyperactive and aggressive symptomatology in predicting adolescent outcome among hyperactive children. *Journal of Pediatric Psychology, 4,* 93–112.

Quinn, P. O. (1994). What is attention deficit disorder? In P. O. Quinn (Ed.), *ADD and the college student* (pp. 1–5). New York: Brunner/Mazel.

Robin, A. L. (1994). Adolescent self-report of ADHD symptoms. *The ADHD Report, 2,* 4–6.

Safer, D., & Krager, J. (1994). The increased rate of stimulant treatment for hyperactive/inattentive students in secondary schools. *Pediatrics, 94,* 462–465.

SAT Program—The College Board. (1994). SAT services for students with disabilities: Information for counselors and admissions officers. Princeton, NJ: College Entrance Examination Board.

Weiss, G., & Hechtman, L. T. (1993). *Hyperactive children grown up* (2nd ed.). New York: Guilford Press.

Weiss, G., Minde, K., Werry, J. S., Douglas, V. I., & Nemeth, E. (1971). Studies on the hyperactive child, VIII: Five-year follow-up. *Archives of General Psychiatry, 24,* 409–414.

Wilens, T., & Biederman, J. (1992). The stimulants. *Psychiatric clinics of North America, 15,* 191–221.

Chapter 6

THE POSTSECONDARY STUDENT

By the time students reach the postsecondary level, one would expect that those individuals with ADD would already have been identified. We would further expect that these students, their parents, and the educational system would be well aware of the symptoms of this disorder and be familiar with the appropriate measures that are needed to foster academic success. Unfortunately, that is not the case. Nearly 50% of students seen at the postsecondary level are either being diagnosed with the disorder for the first time or, if previously diagnosed, are facing symptoms that are reemerging in their present environment (Richards, 1994). A good example of the latter situation was presented by a patient I saw just last summer.

> I first diagnosed David as having ADD when he was 5 years old and I worked with him until he was 13. During that time, he was treated with Dexedrine (dextroamphetamine) for his ADD, had periods of counseling including family therapy, and responded to a behavior management program implemented as necessary. He was a bright student and did not need many accommodations in the classroom if he took his medication. David was mainstreamed and basically did very well. As usually happens at the age of 13 or 14, David decided that he no longer needed to take his stimulant medication and that he could do just as well in school without it. He did have some difficulties during his high school career but managed to graduate and was accepted at a prestigious state polytechnic institute.
> David found college to be extremely difficult and received a grade point average (GPA) of 1.20 his freshman year. During his sophomore year, he realized that college took more effort and required better organizational skills and concentration than he possessed. Even with easier courses, he fell behind. At that point he came to me deciding to "reel himself in" and again sought treatment for his ADD, which he now admitted was affecting his achievement. David went on medication and attended summer school, receiving an "A" in that course. The following semester, he felt that things were getting back on track and he was better organized and attentive. His mother recently called to say that he had made the dean's list.

When we look at these students with ADD at the postsecondary level, three features predominate. First, they are usually underachieving and have poor academic performance. They feel dissatisfied with the grades they are receiving, and their test scores do not reflect their knowledge. Second, they all deal with a sense of frustration and overwhelming procrastination. These students have difficulty organizing, prioritizing, and completing tasks on time. Writing papers or completing lengthy assignments are burdens that are frequently dealt with by postponing and waiting to the last minute. Using the pressure of being "under the gun" for meeting a deadline becomes a method of operation that provides the motivation necessary to get going on a task.

Third, these students with ADD, even those without documented learning disabilities, have a great deal of difficulty with reading and reading comprehension. They have problems with both comprehending what they have read and in persevering in their reading. To sit down and read for three hours is almost an impossible task for these students. Many are so distracted, even when they do read, that they are unable to retrieve the material at the end of a chapter.

Before we discuss the impact of these problems in detail, I would like to address the symptoms of ADD as they now appear in the postsecondary student. Young adults with ADD continue to have difficulty with sustained attention, impulse control, decision making, and distractibility. Hyperactivity can also be seen, but this may be "outgrown" by adolescence and appear at this time as fidgety restlessness and/or inability to sit for long periods. Mood changes can be a hallmark of the disorder during adolescence and young adulthood. The student with ADD can be irritable or impatient. Temper outbursts and unpredictable behaviors are also seen (Quinn, 1994).

FOLLOW-UP STUDIES

Follow-up studies indicate that common areas of continued disturbance are both academic and social. In a study conducted by Minde and colleagues (1972), 25% of the group continued to show antisocial behavior, which had been present at the time of initial evaluation; 80% had poor academic functioning. Weiss and coworkers' (1979) initial 10-year follow-up highlighted some of the difficulties students with ADD continue to demonstrate when compared to controls. Fewer hyperactive subjects were still living with their parents (76% versus 95%). They had made more geographic moves (2.8 versus 1.2) and had more car accidents than controls (mean 1.3 versus 0.07). They had completed less school than controls and had failed more grades in elementary and high school. Average grades in high school were also lower and students were expelled more frequently. However, although these students were rated more inferior by teachers this was not the case with employers (Weiss et al., 1978).

DIAGNOSING ADD IN THE COLLEGE STUDENT

The comprehensive interview becomes critical to establishing the diagnosis for the clinician dealing with students in this age group. It is really one of the only ways to obtain information toward the diagnosis, as data from teachers, parents, medical records, and other sources are usually not available. This structured interview presents the opportunity for the clinician to inquire about the symptoms of ADD as they present at this time and how they have affected the student previously. It should also include a full medical and family history inquiring for other neuropsychiatric conditions as well as ADD.

Kathleen Nadeau has developed a checklist especially for students at the postsecondary level. This checklist, previously published in *ADD and the College Student* (Quinn, 1994), is designed to evaluate the various symptoms of ADD and improve the student's self-awareness. It is meant to be used as part of a structured interview and not for self-diagnosis. While many of the symptoms inquired about in this checklist occur in all college-age students to some degree, it is the overall incidence and severity of symptoms that should be considered in making a diagnosis.

COLLEGE LEVEL ADHD QUESTIONNAIRE*

Rate *every* statement by placing the appropriate number that most fits you in the space to the left of each item. If an item does not apply to you (e.g., an item regarding children, if you are not a parent) please write NA for "not applicable."

0—I do not feel this statement describes me at all.

1—I feel this statement describes me to a slight degree.

2—I feel this statement describes me to a moderate degree.

3—I feel this statement describes me to a large degree.

4—I feel this statement describes me to a very large degree.

Inattention

_____ It's hard for me to stick to one thing for long periods of time (except TV, computer games, or socializing).

_____ My parents have complained I don't listen.

_____ I tune in and out during class lectures.

_____ It's hard for me to study for long periods of time.

_____ Sometimes when reading, my eyes are scanning the words, but my mind is somewhere else.

_____ In group situations I sometimes have trouble following the conversation.

Impulsivity

_____ I "got in trouble" in school for talking or misbehaving.

_____ I tend to "go with my feeling" and often don't think before I act.

_____ I interrupt others in conversation.

*From K. Nadeau. (1994). How do you know if you have ADD? In P. O. Quinn (Ed.), *ADD and the College Student* (pp. 7–18). New York: Brunner/Mazel. Reprinted with permission.

_____ Sometimes I hurt people's feelings without meaning to because I speak before I think.

_____ I am a risk-taker.

_____ I make decisions quickly.

_____ When I have a job to do, I just dive in and figure it out as I go.

Hyperactivity

_____ I am a fast eater.

_____ I eat standing up.

_____ Sometimes I bother people around me by tapping, jiggling, or moving.

_____ I have trouble slowing down.

_____ I am very talkative.

_____ I feel bored and impatient frequently.

_____ In class I feel restless and fidgety.

Distractibility

_____ I become easily sidetracked.

_____ I am constantly noticing or thinking of things unrelated to the task I am doing.

_____ I jump from topic to topic in conversation.

_____ It's hard for me to keep track of a project that I need to check on every few hours or days.

_____ I have forgotten someone on "call-waiting" because I became engrossed in conversation on the other line.

_____ If I don't do something when I think of it, I usually forget to do it.

_____ It's very hard for me to study if people are talking nearby.

Hyperfocusing

_____ Sometimes I become so involved in what I'm doing that I completely lose track of time.

_____ People talk to me or call me when I'm engrossed in something and I don't hear them.

Time Management

_____ I have trouble being "on time."

_____ I tend to procrastinate.

_____ I am unrealistic about how long a task will take.

_____ I take on too many projects and then exhaust myself trying to complete them.

_____ I overcommit and then make excuses when I have to break commitments.

_____ My girlfriend/boyfriend gets annoyed because I keep her/him waiting.

Self-Discipline

_____ I rarely keep resolutions I make.

_____ I often stay up too late at night and have trouble getting up in the morning.

_____ I usually do what I like and put off things that I ought to do.

_____ The only way I can get myself to study is to wait until the deadline.

_____ I have taken up and dropped many interests.

_____ I often quit an activity when it becomes difficult.

_____ I have been called lazy.

_____ I have been called irresponsible.

_____ It's hard for me to stay in and study when friends invite me to go out.

_____ I often oversleep.

Organization/Structure

_____ I rarely plan my day.

_____ I tend to be messy.

_____ My messiness has caused conflict with my parents or roommate.

_____ I have trouble keeping up with several simultaneous projects.

_____ I become overwhelmed when I have too many choices.

_____ I have trouble managing money.

_____ I have difficulty keeping my checkbook balanced.

_____ I have had to borrow money from friends or parents because I was in a jam.

_____ I try to get organized, but it never lasts long.

_____ I often turn papers in late.

_____ It's hard for me to prioritize things I need to do.

Stimulants

_____ I drink four or more cups of coffee or cokes a day.

_____ I use No-Doze or other stimulant pills to keep alert.

Substance Abuse

_____ I have used alcohol excessively.

_____ My friends or parents have been concerned about my drinking.

_____ I have used drugs recreationally.

_____ I have experimented with hard drugs.

_____ I have a substance addiction.

Memory

_____ I tend to forget appointments.

_____ I rely on parents, friends, girlfriends/boyfriends to be my reminder.

_____ I tend to misplace personal items.

_____ I lose my car keys.

_____ I forget what my parents or others ask me to do.

_____ It's hard for me to remember things I intend to do.

_____ If I don't write it down, I'll forget it.

_____ Even if I write things down, I often misplace the note.

Frustration Tolerance

_____ I have been called impatient.

_____ I become easily frustrated.

_____ It's hard to tolerate people who do things slowly.

_____ I hate to wait.

Anger

_____ I fought frequently as a child.

_____ I have a short fuse.

_____ If someone raises his/her voice at me, I yell back.

_____ I have punched holes in walls or doors out of anger.

_____ I usually become angry if I am criticized.

_____ It's almost impossible for me to remain calm if someone is acting in an angry manner toward me.

Academics

_____ I have been called an underachiever.

_____ School has seemed boring and frustrating for as long as I can remember.

_____ My grades went down in junior high compared to elementary school.

_____ My siblings were better students than I was.

_____ I was diagnosed with learning problems.

_____ My teachers and parents always felt I was unmotivated in school.

_____ My grades varied from A's to F's.

_____ Low grades were often a result of not turning in homework.

_____ Even when I studied hard for tests, during the exam I "blanked out" and couldn't remember information.

_____ Careless errors have frequently lowered my grades.

Anxiety/Depression

_____ I have had periods when I felt depressed for weeks or months.

_____ I feel so anxious and overwhelmed that I feel like dropping out of school.

_____ I worry a lot about my future.

_____ I'm afraid I'll never "get my act together."

_____ I have occasionally felt suicidal.

_____ Often I drink or party just to get my mind off my troubles.

_____ I have taken medication for anxiety or depression.

_____ I have been in therapy.

_____ Sometimes I can't get out of bed, I feel so overwhelmed.

_____ I have headaches, stomachaches, neckaches, and backaches from tension and worry.

Self-Esteem and Confidence

_____ I tend to put myself down.

_____ I try to avoid competitive situations.

_____ I overreact to criticism.

_____ I can't "take" teasing.

_____ My feelings are easily hurt.

_____ I worry a lot about making mistakes.

_____ I'm always "messing up."

Oppositional Tendencies

_____ I was a "difficult child."

_____ I don't like being told what to do.

_____ I argue a lot.

_____ I have been called stubborn.

_____ I have had many disagreements with my parents.

_____ I have been fired or had arguments with supervisors on jobs.

Social/Interpersonal

_____ I was teased a lot as a kid.

_____ I had trouble getting along with other kids.

_____ I always felt "different" as a child.

_____ I have been called bossy.

_____ Sometimes I am too blunt or critical.

_____ Though I don't mean to be, my roommate or girlfriend/ boyfriend has said I'm inconsiderate.

_____ I have had conflicts with roommates or coworkers.

Family History

_____ There is a history of alcoholism in my family.

_____ There is a history of depression in my family.

_____ Other family members (including cousins, aunts, uncles) have been diagnosed as hyperactive or learning disabled.

_____ One of my parents says he/she was a lot like me when he/she was younger.

MULTIMODAL TREATMENT PROGRAM

Following the observation of significant difficulties and after confirming the diagnosis in the student, the clinician may recommend treatment from a variety of modalities. The treatment of ADD at this level requires a comprehensive program that addresses the medical, educational, psychological, and behavioral needs of the student. The medical treatment of ADD remains an integral and important piece of the program even at this level. However, the student may also need accommodations and adaptations to his or her program that fall into the domain of the disability service provider on campus. Coordination with a team—including mental health professionals, educational specialists, tutors, and counselors—is imperative to ensure success at the postsecondary level.

The student may benefit from individual therapy at this time, but support groups can be extremely effective. It is there that students will learn that they are not alone and that others have done this before them. Support groups can also provide valuable information about campus activities and services, instructors, and curriculum needs. Career counseling, particularly aimed toward choosing a major field of study, is usually necessary as well. Impulsivity and inability to plan ahead to achieve long-range goals usually causes the student either to have difficulty choosing a major or to change majors frequently.

Academic accommodations and modifications described below may be necessary to improve academic performance. The degree to which each student is affected by the symptoms of ADD will vary tremendously. The existence of comorbid conditions and learning disabilities may also alter the picture.

ACCOMMODATIONS AND MODIFICATIONS

Legally, colleges must provide required services at no additional charge to students with disabilities. While the administration must make the necessary adaptations in courses, examinations, and activities to make them accessible to the student, the institution is not required to provide remedial services to improve the skill level of the student (Latham & Latham, 1994). Unlike the secondary school experience where services are provided to the student under the Individual Educational Program (IEP), college students under section 504 of the Rehabilitation Act (RA) (see Chapter 9, on legal rights) must take a more active role. Students now have the responsibility of notifying the appropriate service provider of their disabilities and the accommodations necessary to meet those needs (Brinckerhoff et al., 1992).

Self-awareness is therefore a key to accessing services at the postsecondary level. The institution is responsible for providing the accommodations but the student's responsibility is to make the request. Disclosing a disability is always fraught with uncertainty and anxiety. "In disclosing disabilities and requesting college accommodations, the student should consult with professionals to determine what documentation to provide to the college.... If a student has questions about confidentiality of information regarding the disability, he or she may consult with independent professionals and/or college personnel" (Latham & Latham, 1994).

As a rule, accommodations should provide the student with the structure and assistance necessary to succeed at the postsecondary level. These adaptations should meet the specific needs of the individual student. Guidance as to course requirements and specific expectations should be provided. Students with ADD may need assistance in prioritizing, organizing, and time-management techniques. Accommodations may include several of the following, but by no means should this be considered an exhaustive list:

- Accommodations in courses that might include priority registration, reduced course load, books on tape, priority seating, and course modifications.
- Course substitution for foreign language or math requirement.
- Clarification of assignments with specific feedback from course instructor.
- Use of note taker for class notes.
- Extended time for tests or examinations, with administration in a distraction-free environment, if necessary.
- Extra time for completing writing assignments, with an arrangement to have rough drafts evaluated.
- Change in test format (use of tape recorders or oral examinations).
- Alteration of examination schedule so that the student has more time between examinations or does not have several examinations within a short interval.

Extended time as an accommodation appears to be particularly effective in allowing students with disabilities to reach their potential. The effect of extended time on reading comprehension using the Nelson-Denny Reading Comprehension and Reading Rate Test was investigated by M. K. Runyan (1991). The major findings of this study were that there is a significant difference between scores obtained by students with learning disabilities and normally achieving students under timed conditions and no significant differences in test scores when students with disabilities are given extra time. Normally achieving students did not perform significantly better with extra time.

MEDICATION

Stimulants are by far the most frequently used treatment for ADD and continue to be effective in this population. Methylphenidate and dextroamphetamine are used with great success. However, these medications, although safe and effective, can produce side effects, with some of these side effects being more common than others. Anorexia and insomnia are still frequently seen in this age group. (See Chapter 8, on medication, for further discussion of side effects; prescribing information is also given in that chapter and is therefore not covered here.) Discussion of contraindications to the use of other medications and stimulants—such as caffeine and cocaine—should take place at the time of initial treatment. Alcohol consumption and drug abuse can also be discouraged at that time.

Once established on a stable dose of medication with a good therapeutic response, the student should be followed at regular intervals. If stimulants are prescribed, a quick check can be made monthly as each prescription is refilled. Compliance with dosage schedules can be monitored by keeping track of the frequency of refills. Height, weight, and blood pressure should also be monitored, particularly if significant appetite suppression or weight loss is a problem.

COUNSELING OR PSYCHOTHERAPY

Other treatments should be recommended in conjunction with medication to assure the most positive outcome for students at the postsecondary level. Psychotherapy and supportive counseling are critical in dealing not only with the symptoms of ADD but also with secondary emotional and social issues. Many students with ADD have developed problems with anxiety, depression, low self-esteem, and interpersonal relationships. To succeed at college, the student with ADD must focus on academic pursuits. Struggles with emotional problems, self-doubts, loneliness, or social isolation can make academic tasks more difficult. Counseling as the student makes the transition to college living is strongly suggested (Nadeau, 1994). Counseling may also help the individual address issues of impulse control, decision making, and goal-setting behaviors.

College and career counseling are important, since the student with ADD has more difficulty choosing a major area of study and changes or drops course more frequently. Strategies for better time management including the use of calendars, planners, computer schedules, and reminders—have all proven useful for the student complaining of disorganization.

CONCLUSION

In order to assure success at the postsecondary level, the clinician must be responsive to the multifaceted needs of the student with ADD. Counseling sessions to provide information, guidance, and support for the individual student should be incorporated in any treatment program. Medication continues to be effective in addressing the symptoms in this population with minimal side effects. Regular communication between the student, clinician, and disability service director on campus will also be necessary to assist in providing a well-coordinated program. As a student relates in *ADD and the College Student*, "ADD is not a 'life sentence' but part of a 'life style' that requires some adaptations to direct [the student's] life toward achievable, realistic goals" (McCormick, 1994, p. 83).

RESOURCES

Books and articles of related interest are:

ADD and the College Student: A Guide for High School and College Students with Attention Deficit Disorder by Patricia O. Quinn (Ed.), 1994, New York: Brunner/Mazel. (800-825-3089), 128 pages, $13.95.

Survival Guide for College Students with ADD or LD by Kathleen Nadeau, 1994, New York: Brunner/Mazel. (800-825-3089), 64 pages, $9.95.

Promoting Postsecondary Education for Students with Learning Disabilities by Loring Brinckerhoff, Stan Shaw, and Joan McGuire, 1993, Austin, TX: Pro-Ed. (512-451-3246), 440 pages, $41.00.

Unlocking Potential: College and Other Choices for Learning Disabled People—A Step-by-Step Guide by Barbara Scheiber and Jeanne Talpers, 1987, Chevy Chase, MD: Adler & Adler. (301-654-4271), 204 pages, $12.95.

Higher Education Services for Students with Attention Deficit Disorder and Learning Disabilities: A Legal Guide by Patricia H. Latham and Peter S. Latham, 1994, Cabin John, MD: National Center for Law and Learning Disabilities. (301-469-8308), 32 pages, $18.00.

Journal of Postsecondary Education and Disability, Vol 2, Nos. 2 and 3, 1995, Columbus, OH: Association on Higher Education and Disability. This is a special issue on ADD. The last chapter contains an annotated bibliography by Richard Goldhammer.

Organizations that may be useful to the student or clinician:

AHEAD (Association for Higher Education and Disability)
P.O. Box 21192
Columbus, OH 43221
(614-488-4972)

HEATH Resource Center (National Clearinghouse on Postsecondary Education for Individuals with Disabilities)
One Dupont Circle, Suite 800
Washington, D.C. 20036

REFERENCES

Brinckerhoff, L. C., Shaw, S. F., & McGuire, J. M. (1992). Promoting access, accommodations, and independence for college students with learning disabilities. *Journal of Learning Disabilities, 25,* 417–429.

Latham, P. H., & Latham, P. S. (1994). *Higher education services for students with attention deficit disorder and learning disabilities: A legal guide.* Cabin John, MD: National Center for Law and Learning Disabilities.

Latham, P. H., Latham, P. S., Nadeau, K., et al. (1994). College and the student with ADD. Presented at the 6th annual international CH.A.D.D. conference, New York.

McCormick, A. (1994). Learning accommodations for ADD students. In P. O. Quinn (Ed.), *ADD and the college student* (pp. 75–83). New York: Brunner/Mazel.

Minde, K., Weiss, G., & Mendelson, N. (1972). A five-year follow-up study of 91 hyperactive children. *Journal of the American Academy of Child Psychiatry, 11,* 595–610.

Nadeau, K. G. (1994). *Survival guide for college students with ADD or LD.* New York: Brunner/Mazel.

Quinn, P. O. (Ed.). (1994). *ADD and the college student.* New York: Brunner/Mazel.

Quinn, P. O. (1995). Role of the physician and medication issues in the treatment of ADD in postsecondary students. *Journal of Postsecondary Education and Disability, 11,* 44–52.

Richard, M. M. (1992). Considering student support services in college selection. *CHADDER, 5,* 1, 6, 7.

Runyan, M. K. (1991). The effect of extra time on reading comprehension scores for university students with and without learning disabilities. *Journal of Learning Disabilities, 24,* 104–108.

Weiss, G., Hechtman, L., & Perlman, T. (1978). Hyperactives as young adults: School, employer, and self-rating scales obtained during ten-year follow-up evaluation. *American Journal of Orthopsychiatry, 48,* 438–445.

Weiss, G., Hechtman, L. T., Perlman, T., et al. (1979). Hyperactives as young adults: A controlled prospective 10-year follow-up of the psychiatric status of 75 children. *Archives of General Psychiatry, 36,* 675–681.

Chapter 7

ADULTS WITH ADD

As we have seen, ADD begins in early childhood and was initially thought to be outgrown by adolescence. However, we now know that this is not the case, and that while from 30 to 40% of adults are asymptomatic, 40% to 50% of individuals with ADD continue to be bothered by significant symptoms into adulthood. This includes 10 to 15% of adults with ADD whose symptoms can be rated as severe.

The following two cases are typical presentations of adults with ADD, with both individuals gaining awareness of their disorder through the diagnosis and treatment of their children.

Mrs. A's case resembles that of countless other adult women with ADD. She reports that she went to a small private school that was actually ideal for a girl with ADD. There was little homework and she did not really learn any study skills. Class notes were typed out and given to all the students. She had a photographic memory, so she just memorized everything. She made straight "A"s and was a stellar student, even skipping a grade. By the time she graduated from eighth grade, she had won numerous awards in English, French, and sports.

For high school, she attended a prestigious private academy. Her ADD caught up with her there, as she had to take notes. She did manage, but her notes were very disorganized. She still maintained a 3.0 GPA but her main problem was in writing reports. When long-term projects were assigned, she had a great deal of difficulty deciding what topic to choose. She still remembers a science project that caused her great difficulty. She could not settle on a topic and was finally able to do so only with the help of a friend, but she had trouble organizing the amount of work necessary. She waited until the last minute and the night before she hardly slept. She received a "C-" on the project—the worst grade that she had ever received.

With regret, she also recalls two other projects, one in physical science and the other an English paper that all seniors were required to write before graduating. She now admits that she plagiarized both. This seemed easier to her than the overwhelming task of writing a long, structured paper. Because she was a "good girl" no one suspected that she would ever do something so dishonest. She somehow was able to rationalize this even though she now admits that she knew it was wrong at the time. She then spent a good deal of time worrying about getting caught. Reflecting on it now, she feels that if she had spent the time studying, her papers would have been great.

Her college experience was similar to high school. She coasted, with very little studying. She attended a large public university and had a great time but did not apply herself. She always had trouble with reports and would procrastinate and never start until the last minute. Although this is common to some extent with all college students, she remembers that it was really " a *big* deal to have to write a paper." She got married after her junior year. Fortunately, her husband was an excellent writer and he used to help her with all of her papers.

ADD did not have a profound effect on her until later in life. Her house was never really organized and the only time it would really be clean was when company was coming over. She injected structure into her life by the schedules of her husband and children. Her husband would always come home at 6:00 P.M. and half an hour before he arrived she would make sure that the house was straightened. Her days revolved around her young children's nap and preschool schedules. She found that she could get a great deal accomplished if she had these time frames to work around. She could paint an entire room in two hours if that was how long nap time was. She really started to have difficulty when two of her main time structures changed. Her husband went into business for himself and his hours became unpredictable. As she previously had organized her day around his, this was devastating. Other changes occurring at the same time were equally distressing. Her children both went to school all day now and she had quit her part-time job when her husband started his own business. She now had huge blocks of unstructured time. She just could not organize her day. She could see lots of things that needed to be done but she would start one job, see something else that needed to be done, stop what she was doing, and start something else. She basically would not get a lot done and she now had more free time than ever. At that point her son, now a first-grader, was diagnosed with ADD, and she began to entertain the possibility of the diagnosis for herself as well.

Frankie, another adult with ADD, had more difficulty from early childhood. He remembers always being in trouble but not being exactly sure why. When he began attending Catholic elementary school with classrooms of 35 to 40 other children, it was virtually impossible for him to sit still. His first year in school was a disaster and he was asked to repeat first grade because he was "immature and disruptive." Frankie had difficulty concentrating and therefore had difficulty learning to read. Although he was overly active at inappropriate times, he was shy and quiet when it was time to read or otherwise participate in class. Frankie ultimately survived with the help of the "good nuns" and even succeeded in school, but not without long hours of study and struggle. Nothing came easily to him.

Upon graduation from grade school, Frankie was accepted into the freshman class of a prestigious high school. The school, however, accepted him provisionally because he had performed so poorly on the entrance examination. Frankie's inability to focus and concentrate for a full two-hour exam obviously lowered his score. When the administrators went over the exam orally with him, Frankie was able to answer almost all of the questions he had missed. This reflected his ability to do well in oral discussions and short quizzes but not on longer tests covering a great deal of material.

After three months of high school, Frankie, through many hours of hard work, made second honors, and was removed from the provisional list of students. This was not the end of his problems. His "pent up energy" dictated his study habits. Because of his inability to study sitting at a desk for very long, he studied while pacing around his room. This added hours to his study time, but it was the only way he could do his work and not "go crazy." Many Latin, Greek, and English vocabulary lists were learned in this unorthodox manner. The weekly

English composition was written at 5 o'clock in the morning on the day that it was due. Most other written assignments were done at the last minute.

Frankie's participation in the school's athletic program motivated and in the end saved him as a student. Playing football and basketball helped burn off his excess energy and provided Frankie with additional motivation for doing well in school. Frankie periodically made second honors—ironically only when he was participating in sports.

Frankie performed well enough academically and athletically to receive a football scholarship to college. Frankie's study habits, walking around and leaving written assignments to the last possible minute, persisted throughout his college days. His participation in sports again acted as a release and motivation. He performed well enough to be accepted into law school. Law school proved difficult, since it entailed long hours of sitting at a desk and provided no athletic outlet. Frankie lasted one year and then left. Whenever Frankie meets a lawyer now and mulls over the many hours he would have had to put in behind a desk, he cringes and sighs. ·

Obviously any job or profession that required long hours at a desk was not for Frankie. Initially he became a high school teacher and coach. After several years in this position, Frankie joined the ranks of the Federal Bureau of Investigation (FBI) as a special agent. Both of these professions allowed him a great deal of physical activity and movement. His position as a special agent imposed upon him both the structure and discipline that he needed. Because of this Frankie thrived, did well professionally, and enjoyed these positions. The time he had to spend sitting at a desk handling the necessary paperwork presented the only problem. Frankie consistently shied away from promotions to higher positions because of the increased administrative "desk work" and confinement that they entailed.

To this day, Frankie, now in his late fifties, still has trouble sitting down at a desk and concentrating for long periods of time. Whether he is writing letters, preparing tax returns, or paying bills, Frankie still struggles. He never outgrew his problems. In some ways they may be more bothersome now than when he was younger. He has tried both Ritalin (methylphenidate) and Dexedrine (dextroamphetamine), but these have not been the answer. At times they seemed to help, but at other times they were ineffectual. The "Frankie" who was always getting into trouble, the struggling student, the professional who chose active life professions, ultimately became Frank the "procrastinator," who never gets anything done.

DIAGNOSIS OF ADD IN ADULTS

The distress and dysfunction in the lives of these two adults is obvious, but how does this lead one to the diagnosis of ADD. After observing continuing symptoms in adults with a previous history of ADD, Wender and coworkers (1985) referred to this syndrome as Attention Deficit Disorder—Residual Type (Wender et al., 1981,1985). Their work led to the establishment of the UTAH criteria for the diagnosis of this disorder and included the following: The individual must have had a history of the disorder in childhood, including symptoms of attention deficit and fidgety, restless behaviors. In addition, the individual might also have had behavior problems, impulsivity, overexcitability, or temper outbursts as a child. As an adult the individual must have symptoms of both persistent motor hyperactivity and attentional deficits. The adult might also experience impulsivity, inability to complete tasks, poor organization, and stress intolerance. Emotional lability may also be reported with hot temper, explosive, or short-lived outbursts.

The *Diagnostic and Statistical Manual of Mental Disorders*, 3rd ed. (DSM-III), published by the American Psychiatric Association (1980) first used the term *Attention Deficit Disorder, Residual Type* (314.8). It stated further that the individual must have at one time met the criteria for ADD with hyperactivity, but that signs of hyperactivity may no longer be present. Other symptoms may have persisted into adulthood. These symptoms must have resulted in some impairment of social or occupational functioning, and the disorder could not be due to other causes.

This diagnosis was not listed in the DSM III-R published in 1987, and the DSM-IV (1994) criteria offered no separate listing for residual type. However, it divided ADHD into three categories: (1) ADHD, Predominantly Inattentive Type; (2) ADHD, Predominantly Hyperactive-Impulsive Type; and (3) ADHD, Combined Type. DSM-IV did add a coding note stating that adolescents and adults who currently have symptoms of ADHD that no longer meet the full criteria should be diagnosed according to the new categories but the term "in partial remission" should be added.

Hallowell and Ratey (1994) have also suggested diagnostic criteria for ADD in adults. The criteria reflect behaviors that are seen more frequently in individuals with ADD than in others of the same mental age and reflect chronic disturbance in at least 15 of the 20 suggested areas. These areas include a sense of underachievement, difficulty getting organized, chronic procrastination, and trouble following through on tasks or projects. Impulsivity, including impatience and a tendency to say whatever comes to mind, easy distractibility, and restlessness are listed. Mood swings, a tendency to worry, or a sense of insecurity or poor self-esteem are used to address the emotional aspects of ADD. An intolerance of boredom and a search for high stimulation are listed along with a tendency toward addictive behavior. Individuals with ADD are reported to be creative, intuitive, or highly intelligent but can have poor self-observation. A family history of ADD, manic-depressive illness, depression, or substance abuse may also be seen. As with the other criteria used in the diagnostic process, in addition to the above symptoms, adults with ADD must have a childhood history of ADD and the situation cannot be explained by other medical or psychiatric conditions.

FOLLOW-UP STUDIES

Studies that have followed children diagnosed with ADD into adulthood have found a persistence of symptoms, with less stability and satisfaction in areas such as educational achievement, employment, and interpersonal relationships. Underachieving and impulsivity with emotional lability were also reported (Weiss & Hechtman, 1993; Mannuzza et al., 1993). In their 15-year prospective follow-up study of the children diagnosed at the Montreal Children's Hospital as having been hyperactive, Weiss and coworkers found that 66% of the hyperactives as adults complained of at least one of the symptoms of ADD, versus 7% of controls. Significantly more adults in the hyperactive group complained of feeling restless, and 44% of the group were actually rated as restless during a structured psychiatric interview versus 9.7% for controls. No differences were found between subjects of the study and controls for somatic or psychotic symptoms and autonomy-related problems. There was a significant difference for neurotic and interpersonal problems in the hyperactives as adults. There was also a trend for the hyperactives to have been more aggressive over the preceding three years, but there was not more verbal aggression. Incidence of suicide attempts was also significantly increased for the follow-up group. This study suggested that hyperactives were not significantly different from controls on measures of drug and alcohol use and antisocial behavior. For a more in-depth report of this 15-year follow-up study, the reader is referred to *Hyperactive Chil-*

dren Grown Up by Weiss and Hechtman (1993), which elaborates on these and several other areas.

DIAGNOSING ADD IN ADULTS

Lynn Weiss, in her book *ADD in Adults,* succinctly explains how ADD is manifested in her patients:

> My adult patients with ADD complain of an inability to cope with the stresses of life. They complain of chronic and unspecified emotional pain, and ... they may experience deep depression over their unfulfilled potential. Their frustration and uncontrolled temper may show up as child or spouse abuse or be expressed in other criminal acts. Friendships and family relations are rocky and often fail. (Weiss, 1992, p. 21)

Dissatisfaction with their place in life appears to be one of the hallmarks of adults with ADD. They could have gotten better grades or gone further in school. Career advancement appears to have been stymied and the adult with ADD always feels that he or she could have done better. Adults with ADD change jobs and "drop out" more frequently. They characteristically perceive themselves as not having achieved as much success or received as much education as their siblings. Family discord is prevalent and adults with ADD have difficulty maintaining stable relationships.

Attention deficits persist and show up during tasks that are of low interest or tedious. Highly motivating or interesting tasks may not produce the same response. These deficits are also affected adversely by environmental conditions and may manifest under certain conditions and not others. Therefore, Attention Deficit Disorder in adults is difficult to diagnose.

The criteria presented in the beginning of this chapter are

useful tools in establishing the diagnosis, but whether the clinician chooses to use DSM-IV, Wender's Utah criteria, or those of Hallowell and Ratey, it is necessary to conduct direct observational interviews with the adult as well as the family or significant other. In addition, in order to meet the criteria for diagnosis, it is required that adults with ADD have had symptoms that presented before the age of 7. Frequently it is difficult for adults to remember what they were like as children. To address this issue, Wender, in his book *The Hyperactive Child, Adolescent, and Adult* (1987), states that in his research he has dealt with this problem in two ways. First, he has encouraged his patients to discuss with their parents the problems that they had during childhood. He then may request that parents fill out questionnaires regarding the characteristics of the adult patient when he or she was a child. Wender further recommends that a spouse, significant other, or parent participate to some degree in the diagnostic process.

QUESTIONNAIRES

Questionnaires are now available that aid in the structured interview process. These can also be useful tools in establishing the diagnosis of ADHD. Barkley has developed an excellent workbook for clinicians entitled *Attention-Deficit Hyperactivity Disorder: A Clinical Workbook* (1991). In this workbook, interview forms and rating scales are provided. These are used in the adult ADHD clinic at the University of Massachusetts Medical Center for evaluating adult referrals to the clinic. Permission is given to photocopy these pages for personal use. Forms include a semistructured interview that inquires about current symptoms, past history (medical and psychiatric), current medications, family history, and social history. Also provided are a series of self-rating checklists. These include a self-rating symptom checklist, a physical complaints checklist, and a patient's behavior checklist. These forms may be useful in providing a framework for clinicians to obtain background information, elicit symptoms, and establish a baseline against which to evaluate the success of various treatment interventions.

Conners also has a *Conners Adult ADHD History Form* (1995) that is designed to be given to patients prior to the first visit, which covers historical information, relevant medical information, family, past school, and employment histories, as well as a description of the current problem.

The Attention-Deficit Scales for Adults (ADSA) has recently been developed by Santo Triolo to aid clinicians in the assessment and diagnosis of ADD in adults. This instrument seems to have a high degree of accuracy in differentiating those adults with ADD from those who do not meet the clinical criteria for the disorder. In addition, *Attention-Deficit Scales for Adults (ADSA)* include *The Manual for Scoring and Interpretation* (coauthored with Kevin Murphy).

Brown's *Attention-Deficit Disorder Scales* are also available for use in ADD assessment. This 40-item self-report for adults (there is also a scale tailored for use with adolescents) is designed to be administered in 20 to 40 minutes within an interview format. The Brown Scales also include a Diagnostic Form, which contains a complete set of protocols and forms necessary for the comprehensive evaluation of possible ADD in adults 18 years or older.

Other scales to aid adults in self-assessment include the *Adult ADD Questionnaire* (1995) by Kathleen Nadeau and the *Copeland Symptom Checklist for Adult Attention Deficit Disorders* (1994) by Edna Copeland.

Physical Examination and Routine Tests

A complete physical examination should be performed on all individuals suspected of having ADD to rule out other causes of the presenting symptoms (e.g., hypoglycemia, drug abuse, epilepsy, hyperthyroidism, anxiety, mania, or stress). Prior to instituting any medical interventions, it is also critical to establish the presence of other medical conditions such as hypertension, allergies, asthma, headaches, or cardiac disease. Brain scans or electroencephalograms are not necessary as part of a routine evaluation for ADD. However, a vision and hearing screening as well as routine blood testing should be performed. These blood tests should include thyroid studies, as ADD has been associated in children (70%) and adults (50%) with generalized resistance to thyroid hormone (Hauser et al., 1993).

COMORBID CONDITIONS

Individuals with ADD have been found to have comorbid conditions in as many as 40% of cases. These include Obsessive-Compulsive Disorder (OCD) (Rapoport, 1986), anxiety disorders, depression, oppositional or conduct disorders (Beiderman et al., 1991; Pliszka, 1992), and tics or Tourette's syndrome (Comings & Comings, 1984). The clinician must be aware of the presence of these comorbid disorders in the adult seeking diagnosis for ADD or be sure that these conditions are ruled out when making the diagnosis. In a sample of 56 adults with ADD, 53% were diagnosed as having a general anxiety disorder, 34% alcohol abuse or dependence, 30% drug abuse, 25% dysthymic disorder, and 25% cyclothymic disorder (Shekim et al., 1990).

In addition, a large percentage of individuals with ADD also have learning disabilities (LD) (Barkley, 1990) or impulsive cognitive styles (Hopkins et al., 1979). Upon testing these cognitive styles placed the adults with ADD at a disadvantage in choosing an alternative in situations where the response was uncertain and when they had to select the relevant aspects of a complex stimulus. They are more easily distracted by irrelevant stimuli and less able to inhibit incorrect verbalizations. The clinician should be sure that these areas have been addressed by conducting thorough educational and psychological assessments or by making the referral for a complete neuropsychological evaluation if this has not already been performed.

Denckla (1991) proposes that selected neuropsychological batteries assessing the domain of executive function offer opportunities to document the cognitive correlates of ADD and the several facets of attention that are affected. She further suggests that these test results provide clues to the neurobiological foundation of ADD and its response to therapeutic intervention. Results of preliminary studies indicate that stimulant medication improves aspects of executive function, including inhibition and sustaining attention, but not planning and organization. Significant improvements were also seen on continuous performance and verbal fluency tests. The diagnosis of ADD in adults, however, does not depend on the results of this testing and for the present remains a purely historical diagnosis requiring some degree of treatment in most cases.

MULTIMODAL TREATMENT PROGRAM

As with all other complex disorders, treatment of ADD in adults must involve a well-coordinated program including education, medication, therapy, and specific accommodations to address symptomatology.

ADULT EDUCATION

There are now several popular books and videos available for the adult with ADD. A sampling of these follows.

Books

Driven to Distraction by Edward Hallowell and John Ratey, 1994, New York: Pantheon Press. 319 pages, $23.00.

Answers to Distraction by Edward Hallowell and John Ratey, 1994, New York: Pantheon Books. 334 pages, $21.00.

You Mean I'm Not Lazy, Stupid, or Crazy?! by Kate Kelly and Peggy Ramundo, 1995, New York: Scribner. 465 pages, $19.95.

Attention Deficit Disorder in Adults by Lynn Weiss, 1992, Dallas, TX: Taylor. 217 pages, $19.95.

The Hyperactive Child, Adolescent, and Adult by Paul Wender, 1987, New York: Oxford University Press. 162 pages, $10.95.

Women with Attention Deficit Disorder by Sari Solden, 1995, Grass Valley, CA: Underwood Books. 288 pages, $11.95.

A Comprehensive Guide to Attention Deficit Disorder in Adults: Research, Diagnosis, and Treatment by Kathleen Nadeau (Ed.), 1995, New York: Brunner/Mazel. 320 pages, $38.95.

Adventures in Fast Forward: Life, Love, and Work for the ADD Adult by Kathleen Nadeau, 1996, New York: Brunner/Mazel. 210 pages, $18.95.

Hyperactive Children Grown Up, 2nd edition, by Gabrielle Weiss and Lily Hechtman, 1993, New York: Guilford Press. 473 pages, $19.95.

Attention Deficit Disorder: A Different Perception by Thom Hartmann, 1993, Penn Valley, CA: Underwood Books. 163 pages, $9.95.

Out of the Fog: Treatment Options and Coping Strategies for Adult Attention Deficit Disorder by Kevin Murphy and Susan LeVert, 1995, New York: Hyperion. 320 pages, $13.00.

Videos

ADHD in Adults by Russell Barkley, New York: Guilford Press Videos, Guilford Publications. (800-365-7006), $95.00.

Adults with Attention Deficit Disorder: ADD Isn't Just Kid's Stuff by Thomas Phelan, Glen Ellyn, IL: Child Management. (800-442-4453), $45.00.

ADHD in Adulthood by Arthur Robin, Worcester, MA: Professional Advancement Seminars. (508-792-2408), $59.00.

Support Groups and Newsletters

CH.A.D.D. (Children and Adults with Attention Deficit Disorder), 499 NW 70th Avenue, Plantation, FL 33317, (305-587-3700).

ADDA. (The National Attention Deficit Disorder Foundation), P.O. Box 972, Mentor, OH 44063, (800-487-2282).

ADDendum (quarterly newsletter), c/o Beverly Horn, 5041-A Backlick Road, Annandale, VA 22003.

ADDult News. (published and edited by Mary Jane Johnson, President of ADDA), 2620 Ivy Place, Toledo, OH 43613.

Challenge. P.O. Box 448, West Newbury, MA 01985.

MEDICATION

Stimulants are as effective in adults with ADD as in other age groups and can, contrary to popular belief, be used in these populations (Wood et al., 1976; Wender et al., 1985). Higher doses of stimulants may be necessary in this population, with best results occurring at a level of 1.0 mg/kg/day. This correlates somewhat with the need for moderate- (20 mg/day) and higher-dose (30 mg/day) methylphenidate treatment in 71% of the subjects with ADHD reported by Barkley and coworkers in 1991. In this sample, 95% of patients were found to be positive responders to the stimulant medication used (Barkley et al., 1991).

Methylphenidate (Ritalin) is the most commonly used medication for ADD. Dextroamphetamine (Dexedrine) is also used, particularly in adults. If there is no response to the initial stimulant medication prescribed than the other should be tried (Elia & Rapoport, 1991).

Tricyclic antidepressants can also be used, and blood tests are available to determine if levels are in the therapeutic range. However, the practitioner should be aware that there is controversy regarding the optimal doses of the tricyclics in adults; readers are referred to the discussion of this topic in Chapter 8. Other antidepressants such as fenfluramine, fluoxetine, and sertraline have also been used. These, however, have not been shown to be effective in addressing the core symptoms of attention, impulsivity, and hyperactivity, and they work better in combination with the stimulants in addressing comorbid conditions such as depression.

Combination therapies are more frequently being advocated for adults with ADD. Beta-adrenergic blockers (Ratey et al., 1991) and the noradrenergic agonist clonidine (Hunt et al., 1985) when paired with the stimulants, appear to enhance the overall attentional and organizational effects of the stimulant medication and alleviate the insomnia, irritability, and impulsiveness.

ACCOMMODATIONS IN THE WORKPLACE

Many adults with ADD do not complain of inattention in the workplace. This is because they have either "outgrown" the symptom or have found employment that allows them to shift attention frequently or delegate to others assignments that require a great deal of attention. However, some adults do continue to have problems with distractibility, restlessness, and poor time management in the workplace. For this group, accommodations may be necessary to address the symptoms of ADD as they now impact on functioning. These may include requesting use of a private office or a work space that is less distracting, having instructions written down or explained thoroughly, developing timetables for breaking down tasks into smaller segments, tape recording important meetings or instructions, using a computerized planner or organizer, receiving more frequent feedback from supervisors, or hiring additional clerical personnel to assist with the details of a task.

However, even with such accommodations available, it should be kept in mind that while accommodations may be useful to maximize job performance, it is the responsibility of the adult with ADD to find a good job match. Information regarding "finding that job," "getting the job," and what to do "on the job" is discussed along with the legal rights of the individual in Patricia and Peter Latham's *Succeeding in the Workplace, Attention Deficit Disorder and Learning Disabilities in the Workplace: A Guide for Success* (1994).

THERAPY

Adults with ADD benefit from both individual and group therapy. In addition, they have stated, when questioned, that cognitive training is also effective in dealing with some of the symptoms of ADD. Adults with ADD can benefit from time-management training or memory-enhancing strategies, and vocational counseling is imperative for the adult who is seeking to pursue higher education or a career change.

Individual psychotherapy is quite useful for adults dealing with the symptoms of ADD. Usually the adult will begin therapy in an effort to explain symptoms and deal with current problems. Depression, marital and family conflicts, and substance abuse may have driven such individuals to seek help, not suspecting that ADD may be the cause of many of their difficulties. Education regarding the symptoms of ADD and its diagnosis along with any comorbid conditions can help these adults deal more effectively with their situation. Knowledge about the disorder can save marriages and improve relationships. The spouse must be involved actively in the processes of both diagnosis and treatment.

Family therapy and couples sessions are critical to restore some balance in these relationships. Hallowell presents 25 tips on the management of ADD in couples which clinicians may find useful if they will be doing the couples therapy themselves (Hallowell, 1993). If children in the family also have ADD, parenting skills may have to be addressed to help the adults deal more effectively with compliance issues. Conflict-resolution therapy with adolescents seems to be particularly effective (Robin & Foster, 1989).

Group therapy for adults with ADD may be useful to provide insight and to teach organizational or social skills. Vocational counseling and support for adults to continue their education or to change careers is also important. Many adults with ADD and learning disabilities wish to return to complete the college education that they were forced to give up years ago.

CONCLUSION

ADD in adults, once it is diagnosed, is a very treatable condition. Outcomes can be improved, and with adaptations and accommodations, these individuals can direct their own lives toward achievable, realistic goals. A combination of education, improved self-awareness, family and employer support, and medication may be all that is necessary for success.

REFERENCES

American Psychiatric Association. (1980). *Diagnostic and statistical manual of mental disorders* (3rd ed.). Washington, DC: Author.

American Psychiatric Association. (1987). *Diagnostic and statistical manual of mental disorders* (3rd ed., rev.). Washington, DC: Author.

American Psychiatric Association. (1994). *Diagnostic and statistical manual of mental disorders* (4th ed.). Washington, DC: Author.

Barkley, R. A. (1990). *Attention deficit hyperactivity disorder: A handbook for diagnosis and treatment.* New York: Guilford Press.

Barkley, R. A. (1991). *Attention deficit hyperactivity disorder: A clinical workbook.* New York: Guilford Press.

Barkley, R. A., DuPaul, G. J., & McMurray, M. B. (1991). Attention deficit disorder with and without hyperactivity: Clinical response to three dose levels of methylphenidate. *Pediatrics, 87,* 519–531.

Biederman, J., Faraone, S. B., Keenan, K., & Tsaung, M. T. (1991). Evidence of familial association between attention deficit disorder and major affective disorder. *Archives of General Psychiatry, 48,* 633–642.

Biederman, J., Newcorn, J., & Sprich, S. (1991). Comorbidity of attention deficit hyperactivity disorder with conduct, depressive, anxiety, and other disorders. *American Journal of Psychiatry, 148,* 564–577.

Brown, T. E. (1995). *Brown attention deficit disorder scales.* San Antonio, TX: The Psychological Corporation.

Comings, D. E., & Comings, B. G. (1984). Tourette's syndrome and attention deficit disorder with hyperactivity: Are they related? *Journal of the American Medical Association, 23,* 138–146.

Conners, K. *Conners adult ADHD history form.* (1995). North Tonawanda, NY: Multi-Health Systems.

Copeland, E. D. *Copeland symptom checklist for adult attention deficit disorder.* Macon, GA: MCCG Institute for Developmental Medicine.

Denckla, M. B. (1991). Attention deficit hyperactivity disorder residual type. *Journal of Child Neurology, 6,* Suppl., S44–S50.

Elia, J., & Rapoport, J. (1991). Methylphenidate versus dextroamphetamine: Why both should be tried. In B. Osman & L. L. Greenhill (Eds)., *Ritalin: Theory and patient management* (pp. 243–265). New York: Mary Ann Libert.

Hallowell, E. M. (1993). Living and loving with attention deficit disorder: Couples where one partner has ADD. *CHADDER*, (Spring/Summer), 13–19.

Hallowell, E. M., & Ratey, J. J. (1994). *Driven to distraction*. New York: Pantheon Books.

Hauser, P., Zametkin, A. J., Martinez, P., et al. (1993). Attention deficit hyperactivity disorder in people with generalized resistance to thyroid hormone. *New England Journal of Medicine*, *328*, 997–1001.

Hopkins, J., Perlman, T., Hechtman, L., & Weiss, G. (1979). Cognitive style in adults originally diagnosed as hyperactives. *Journal of Child Psychology and Psychiatry*, *20*, 209–216.

Hunt, R., Minderaa, R., & Cohen, D. (1985). Clonidine benefits children with attention deficit disorder and hyperactivity: Report of a double-blind placebo-crossover therapeutic trial. *Journal of the American Academy of Child and Adolescent Psychiatry*, *24*, 617–629.

Hunt, R., Minderaa, R. B., & Cohen, D. J. (1986). The therapeutic effect of clonidine in attention deficit disorder with hyperactivity: A comparison with placebo and methylphenidate. *Psychopharmacology Bulletin*, *22*, 229–236.

Latham, P., & Latham, P. (1994). *Succeeding in the workplace, attention deficit disorder and learning disabilities in the workplace: A guide for success*. Washington, DC: JKL Communications.

Mannuzza, S., Klein, R. G., Besller, A., et al. (1993). Adult outcome of hyperactive boys. *Archives of General Psychiatry*, *50*, 565–576.

Nadeau, K. (1995). *Adult ADHD questionnaire*. Annandale, VA: Chesapeake Psychological Publications.

Pliszka, S. R. (1992). Comorbidity of attention deficit hyperactivity disorder and overanxious disorder. *Journal of the American Academy of Child and Adolescent Psychiatry*, *31*, 197–203.

Rapoport, J. L. (1986). Childhood obsessive–compulsive disorder. *Journal of Child Psychology and Psychiatry*, *27*, 289–295.

Rapoport, J. L. (1989). *The boy who couldn't stop washing*. New York: Dutton.

Ratey, J. J., Greenberg, M. S., & Lindem, K. J. (1991). Combination of treatments for attention deficit hyperactivity disorder in adults. *Journal of Nervous and Mental Disease, 179,* 699–701.

Robin, A. L., & Foster, S. L. (1989). *Negotiating parent–adolescent conflict: A behavioral family systems approach.* New York: Guilford Press.

Shekim, W. O., Asarnow, R. F., Hess, E., et al. (1990). A clinical and demographic profile of a sample of adults with attention deficit hyperactivity disorder, residual state. *Comprehensive Psychiatry, 31,* 416–425.

Triolo, S. J. (1995). *Attention-deficit scales for adults (ADSA).* New York: Brunner/Mazel.

Wender, P. H. (1987). *The hyperactive child, adolescent, and adult.* New York: Oxford University Press.

Wender, P. H., Reimherr, F. W., & Wood, D. R. (1981). Attention deficit disorders (minimal brain dysfunction) in adults. *Archives of General Psychiatry, 38,* 449–456.

Wender, P. H., Reimherr, F. W., Wood, D. R., & Ward, M. (1985). A controlled study of methylphenidate in the treatment of attention deficit disorder, residual type, in adults. *American Journal of Psychiatry, 142,* 547–552.

Weiss, G., & Hechtman, L. T. (1993). *Hyperactive children grown up* (2nd ed.). New York: Guilford Press.

Weiss, L. (1992). *ADD in adults.* Dallas, TX: Taylor.

Wood, D. R., Reimherr, F. W., Wender, P. H., & Johnson, G. E. (1976). Diagnosis and treatment of minimal brain dysfunction in adults. *Archives of General Psychiatry, 33,* 1453–1460.

Chapter 8

MULTIMODAL
TREATMENT OF ADD

Within the framework of this volume, specific chapters have presented a comprehensive treatment program geared to a particular developmental stage. These are also summarized in the last chapter. At this point, I would merely like to touch on some of the specific therapies or recommendations themselves and briefly discuss the concept and efficacy of the multimodal treatment model.

MULTIMODAL TREATMENT

As we have seen, ADD is a very complex disorder and its management requires multiple treatment modalities. The most common therapies include parent and patient education, classroom interventions (including accommodations and/or special educations placements), counseling, behavioral and cognitive therapies, support groups, and medication. It is through these various interventions that we hope to promote improved functioning, as well as family and peer relationships and to empower both the individual and his or her family with the tools for effective adaptation, self-advocacy, and improved outcome.

Various controversial or nonstandard therapies have also been promoted over the years. These have included various dietary manipulations either by elimination diets or supplementation, electroencephalographic (EEG) biofeedback, sensory integration therapy, and vision training. While the discussion of these alternative therapies is not within the scope of this volume, I would refer the reader to an excellent handbook that covers these controversial treatments in detail, *Attention Deficit Disorder and Learning Disabilities: Realities, Myths and Controversial Treatments* by Barbara Ingersoll and Sam Goldstein (1993).

True multimodal programs integrate the educational, psychological, social, and medical aspects of treatment. They also provide for case management, family support, and advocacy on behalf of the individual with ADD. Whether one is treating children or adults with ADD, it is particularly important to keep in mind that successful treatment should also include significant others and family members. In addition, programs for children should be geared to foster normal development and should include interventions directed at removing the problematic behaviors (Culbert et al., 1994). Combination therapies are necessary if we are to address all of the needs of the individual with ADD. Whereas treatment with stimulant medication has been the most common treatment for ADD for many years, studies now indicate that a combination of therapies may prove more effective than a single modality alone. While medication is certainly effective in addressing many of the symptoms of ADD, researchers and clinicians have been debating for years whether pharmacology alone is enough in the treatment of ADD children (Douglas, 1975; Backman & Firestone, 1979).

COUNSELING

Counseling certainly should not be considered a primary treatment modality for the child or adult with ADD, but it can be particularly useful in individual cases as an effective means of addressing secondary or comorbid symptomatology. Anxiety, poor self-esteem, depression, and significant adjustment problems plague the individual with ADD. "Counseling can afford them the opportunity to reduce feelings of helplessness, increase motivation and improve coping skills" (Goldstein & Goldstein, 1990, p. 285).

The individual with ADD is in need of an explanation of and factual information about ADD. Psychotherapy, when used as a cognitive intervention, provides the opportunity to explain and define ADD. Likewise incorporating bibliotherapy can be extremely useful in addressing these needs. Books on ADD are now quite numerous. Several specifically written for the individual with ADD are recommended throughout this book. One can find books that explain ADD to preschoolers *(Shelly the Hyperactive Turtle)*, adolescents *(Adolescents and ADD: Gaining the Advantage)*, or adults (the popular *Driven to Distraction*).

BEHAVIORAL THERAPIES

Behavioral techniques have been used effectively since the 1960s within classrooms and at home to address individual inappropriate behaviors resulting from specific ADD symptoms. The effectiveness of a self-control package for improving behavior within the classroom was demonstrated by Barkley and coworkers (1980). However, while these techniques were effective in improving behavior and attention to task during individual seat work, they were not found to be effective during group instruction (Barkley et al., 1980). In work comparing behavioral versus pharmacologic treatment of ADD boys and their classmates, Loney and colleagues (1979) documented the positive effects of a behavioral program on the behavior of children with hyperactivity as well as on their overactive and average classmates. While statistically significant and similar treatment effects were found for both the group receiving medication and the group undergoing behavioral treatment, only in the behavior group did the treatment also affect classmates' behavior (Loney et al., 1979).

Behavior management is often seen as a more acceptable form of treatment by the parents of children diagnosed with ADD. In a study conducted at the Children's Hospital of Michigan Attention Deficit Disorder Clinic (Liu et al., 1991), mothers were given the choice of three treatment conditions, methylphenidate, behavior modification, or medication plus behavior modification. When asked to rate the acceptability of each treatment, both control and ADD families rated behavior modification as the most acceptable, methylphenidate as the least acceptable, and the combined therapy in between the other two treatments. After 3.5 months of treatment of the children, there was a significant improvement in acceptance of both methylphenidate and the combined treatment. Mothers' knowledge about ADD was also found to be significantly correlated with their acceptance of methylphenidate and the combined treatment.

The combined use of behavioral therapy and methylphenidate has been shown to enhance the effects seen by either treatment alone. In a study of behavioral intervention, probe periods were introduced using placebo and two doses of methylphenidate. The effect of the stimulant medication was reported to be enhanced when administered after, rather than before a 13-week behavioral intervention program instituted at school and at home. Behavioral therapy alone was found to have effects on on-task behavior that were between those effects seen at the two doses of medication used in this study. Only with high dose medication and behavioral therapy were the hyperactive children found to have behavior ratings in the range of nonhyperactive controls (Pelham et al., 1980).

Studies that include medication and parent training interventions have yielded positive results (Horn et al., 1987; Anastopoulos et al., 1991) even in preschoolers (Pisterman et al., 1988). When parents were involved in a positive reward system for the treatment of their children's behaviors in school, not only did classroom behaviors improve but parents' attitude and behaviors toward their children were also noted to change (Goff & Demetral, 1983).

Pelham (1989) in his article entitled, "Behavior Therapy, Behavioral Assessment, and Psychostimulant Medication in the Treatment of Attention Deficit Disorder: An Interactive Approach," reaches two conclusions regarding behavior therapy and stimulants as treatments for ADD. "First, despite the evidence for their effectiveness, both behavior therapy and psychostimulant medication have limitations that mean that neither alone constitutes a *sufficient* or *maximally effective* treatment for ADD. Secondly, each of these treatment modalities has something to offer that can improve the other's effectiveness...." (p. 169) and "Behavior therapy can be combined with psychostimulant medication to yield a treatment that, on the average, is more effective than either component alone in the short term" (Pelham, 1989, p. 173).

Likewise, Ialongo and coworkers (1993), reporting on a 9-month follow-up, found indications that combined therapies (methylphenidate, parent training, and child self-control instruction) produced greater maintenance of treatment gains than medication alone.

Cognitive Therapy

Cognitive therapy as a form of behavior modification is based on the initial work of Luria in the early 1960s. At that time he proposed a three-stage process by which children achieve self-control. Researchers used this concept and applied it to the treatment of ADD children in hopes of reducing impulsive behaviors and improving social skills.

While little effect from this method of treatment could be found in studies measuring cognitive functioning or academic performance, there is some indication that these techniques may have some impact on self-control behaviors in the classroom (Goldstein & Goldstein, 1990; Reid & Borkowski, 1987) and social problem solving. Problems with generalization of skills have been noted (Abikoff & Gittleman, 1985), and further studies are indicated in this area before any firm conclusions can be reached (Abikoff, 1991).

MEDICATION

Medication has long been considered the single most effective treatment for ADD. With at least 750,000 to 1.6 million individuals now taking medication, prescriptions written for the three main stimulant medications (Ritalin, Dexedrine, and Cylert) have tripled from 1990 to 1994.

There are several reasons for this phenomenon. Clinicians are clearly doing a better job of diagnosing children and adults with ADD. Parents and teachers are more aware of the symptoms of the disorder, and more children are coming to the attention of physicians, who are, in turn, better trained and more likely to prescribe medication than in the past. Adults are also seeking treatment for their attentional deficits and other symptoms related to ADD. Prescriptions written for the treatment of adult symptomatology are among the main reasons that sales of medication have increased dramatically.

On the following pages the clinician will find a discussion of the various medications used to treat Attention Deficit Hyperactivity Disorder. Table 3 (on pp. 166–167) provides comprehensive, valuable details about each of the stimulants, tricyclic antidepressants (TCAs), and clonidine.

STIMULANTS

Stimulants are the most commonly recommended treatment for children, adolescents, and adults with ADD (Gittleman, 1980; Dulcan, 1985, 1990; Barkley, 1990). While all of the stimulants have a similar pharmacokinetics effects, methylphenidate is by far the most commonly prescribed with approximately 90% of patients treated with a stimulant medication receiving this medication (Culbert et al., 1994). We know that stimulants are effective in 75 to 85% of the children and 50% of adults for whom they are prescribed. Let us take a look at the symptoms they address.

Methylphenidate (Ritalin)

Methylphenidate (Ritalin) has been shown to have the major effect of improving attention and decreasing activity level whether in the standard form (Barkley, 1977) or sustained-release (Whitehouse, Shah, & Palmer, 1980). It also exerts a significant effect on classroom measures of attention and academic efficiency to a point where scores of children with ADD no longer differ from those of normal children (DuPaul & Rapport, 1993). Auditory attention and processing skills likewise appear to be improved by methylphenidate to levels of nondisabled children (Keith & Engineer, 1991).

Methylphenidate has been found to have only a minor effect on deficient social skills and oppositional/aggressive behaviors (Ullmann & Sleator, 1985). One possible explanation for this may be that whereas methylphenidate was found to affect reaction time, no change was noted on a task measuring higher cortical processes (decision time) (Adams, 1982). Thus, decision making may remain faulty resulting in continuing deficits in social skill areas. Academic achievement is another area where research has yielded few positive results (Barkley & Cunningham, 1978; Barkley, 1979) but controversies surround several research designs and dose responses do not allow us to answer this question fully at this time (Swanson et al., 1991).

Methylphenidate does, however, clearly have positive effects on the mother-child interaction. In studies, children were seen as more compliant with maternal commands while under drug treatment. The mothers were more aware of this compliance and reduced their directedness toward the children. The boys, however, demonstrated a decrease in social interactions, were less talkative, and increased the amount of independent play. Less parental control and supervision of the boys was required while on medication (Cunningham & Barkley, 1978; Barkley & Cunningham, 1979 a, b, 1980; Barkley et al., 1985).

Methylphenidate does not appear to alter the nonverbal creative thinking ability of boys with ADD (Funk et al., 1993), but dose relationships may have some effect on memory and attention versus behavior, with the optimum dose for one negatively affecting the other. The work of Sprague and Sleator (1977) clearly indicates that high doses of stimulants improve behavior but cause poorer memory and attention, which are improved at a low dose. Barkley and coworkers in 1991 again looked at the dose response of methylphenidate in children with ADD with and without hyperactivity. In this study, it was noted that all children responded positively to three doses of methylphenidate (5, 10, or 15 mg twice a day) as measured on parent and teacher rating scales. The groups were not found to differ significantly on any measures in their response to methylphenidate. However, more children with ADD with-

TABLE 3
Medications for Attention Deficit Hyperactivity Disorders

Name	Cost (approximate)	Dose Schedule	Dose Range	Onset/ Duration	Potential Side Effects
Methylphenidate (Ritalin) 5, 10, 20 mg tablets	$.35 @ 10 mg tablet (generic) $.60 @ 10 mg tablet (brand)	Begin with 5 mg in morning daily. Increase by 5 mg weekly as needed. Usually needs two or three doses/day. Generic dose may differ.	5–80 mg/day	Takes effect in 30 minutes. Lasts about 3–5 hours.	Loss of appetite, weight loss, insomnia, stomachaches, irritability, headaches, social withdrawal, tics, "rebound." Avoid decongestants.
Ritalin SR 20 mg sustained release tablets only	$1.10 @ 20 mg tablet (brand)	Begin with 20 mg in morning daily. Increase by 20 mg as needed. Often needs short-acting tablet in morning to "jump start." Usually given as one to two doses/day.	20–80 mg/day	Takes effect in 60–90 minutes. Lasts about 6–8 hours.	Loss of appetite, weight loss, insomnia, stomachaches, irritability, headaches, social withdrawai, tics, "rebound." Avoid decongestants. Not as potent as regular.
Dextramphetamine (Dexedrine) 5 mg tablets only (Dextrostat) 5, 10 mg tablets	$.25 @ 5 mg tablet	Begin with 2.5 mg in morning daily. Increase weekly by 5 mg as needed. Usually given as two or three dose/day. Elixir no longer available.	2.5–40 mg/day	Takes effect in 30 minutes. Lasts about 3–5 hours.	Loss of appetite, weight loss, insomnia, stomachaches, irritability, headaches, social withdrawal, tics, "rebound." Avoid decongestants.
Dexedrine Spansules 5, 10, 15 mg capsules	$.50 @ 5 mg capsule (brand)	Begin with 5 mg in morning daily. Increase by 5 mg as needed. Given as one to two doses/day.	5–40 mg/day	Takes effect in 60 minutes. Lasts about 6–10 hours.	Loss of appetite, weight loss, insomnia, stomachaches, irritability, headaches, social withdrawal, tics, "rebound." Avoid decongestants.
Bupropion (Wellbutrin) 75, 100 mg	$.70 @ 75 mg	Begin with 75 mg twice a day. Increase to three times a day if needed.	150–300 mg/day	Takes several days to take effect.	Agitation, dry mouth, insomnia, headaches, nausea, constipation, tremor. Avoid in patients with seizures or bulimia.

Medication	Price	Dosing	mg/day	Onset/Duration	Side Effects
Pemoline (Cylert) 18, 75, 37.5, 75 mg tablets 37.5 mg chewable tablets	$1.30 @ 37.5 mg tablet (brand)	Begin with 37.5 mg in morning daily. Increase by 18.25 mg weekly as needed. Usually given in one dose/day. Must be taken daily. Stop slowly.	18.75–112.5 mg/day	Takes 2 weeks to take effect. Tablets then last 12–24 hours.	Insomnia, stomachaches, irritability, headaches. Rarely, abnormal liver function tests. Blood tests needed regularly. Avoid decongestants.
Imipramine (Tofranil) 10, 25, 50, 75 mg tablets	$.10 @ 25 mg tablet (generic) $.50 @ 25 mg tablet (brand)	Begin with 25 mg before bedtime. Increase by 25 mg weekly as needed. Given as one or two doses/day. Must be taken daily. Stop slowly.	25–200 mg/day	Takes 5–10 days to take effect. Tablets then last 12–24 hours.	Fatigue, stomach upset, dry mouth, blurry vision, constipation, dizziness, tics. Baseline electrocardiogram recommended.
Desipramine (Norpramin) 10, 25, 50, 75 mg tablets	$.30 @ 25 mg tablet (generic) $.75 @ 25 mg tablet (brand)	Begin with 25 mg in morning. Increase by 25 mg weekly as needed. Given as one or two doses. Must be taken daily. Stop slowly.	25–200 mg/day	Takes 3–5 days to take effect. Tablets then last 12–24 hours.	Fatigue, stomach upset, dry mouth, blurry vision, constipation, dizziness, tics. Baseline electrocardiogram recommended.
Clonidine (Catapres) 0.1, 0.2, 0.3 mg tablets	$.14 @ 0.1 mg tablet (generic) $.60 @ 0.1 mg tablet (brand)	Begin with 0.05 mg (1/2 tablet) before bedtime. Increase by 0.05 mg weekly as needed. Given as two to four doses/day. Must be taken daily. Stop slowly. Sometimes combined with stimulant.	0.1–0.3 mg/day	Takes 2 weeks to take effect. Tablets then last 8–12 hours.	Sleepiness, dizziness, nausea, hypotension.
Catapres TTS 1, 2, 3 (transdermal patches)	$7 @ TTS patch (brand)	Begin with TTS 1 patch (delivers 0.1 mg/day) may increase slowly after 2 weeks as needed. Stop slowly. Sometimes combined with stimulant.	0.1–0.3 mg/day	Takes 2 weeks to take effect. Lasts 5–7 days.	Sleepiness, dizziness, nausea, hypotension. Skin irritation under patch. Not affected by routine bathing.
Guanfacine (Tenex) 1.2 mg tablets	$.70 @ 1 mg tablet (generic) $.90 @ 1 mg tablet (brand)	Begin with 0.5 mg (1/2 tablet) before bedtime increase by 0.5 mg weekly. Give as one to two doses/day.	0.5–2 mg/day	Takes several days to a week to take effect.	Sleepiness, hypotension.

Source: Reprinted with permission from Karen J. Miller, M.D.

out hyperactivity tended to have no clinical response (24%) or to respond better to the low dose (35%). Most of the children with ADD with hyperactivity were found to respond positively to the medication, with 71% given either the moderate or high dose (Barkley, DuPaul, & McMurray, 1991).

In a similar study of children with ADD without hyperactivity, methylphenidate in doses from 0.4 to 1.2 mg/kg/day was noted to improve school grades during the treatment period, with a marked reduction when the medication was withdrawn (Famularo & Fenton, 1987).

In some children with ADD comorbid aggressivity is a complicating factor. Does methylphenidate have an effect on this aggressive symptomatology? Barkley and colleagues (1989) have studied this issue and found that aggressive and nonaggressive children were quite similar in their response to medication. Aggressive children even showed a greater degree of improvement on conduct ratings, which were poorer to begin with than those of the nonaggressive children. A low dose of methylphenidate was also as effective as higher doses.

Methylphenidate appears to continue to be an effective adjunct to the treatment of ADD in adolescents, with higher doses resulting in the most beneficial response in behavioral, academic, and laboratory measures of attention and impulsivity (Brown & Sexson, 1988). Stimulants appear to be both safe and effective in this age group and response to be dose-related. In studies summarized in Wilens and Beiderman (1992), an overall medication response rate of 75% was reported in adolescents.

Studies of methylphenidate in adults also indicate effectiveness but with perhaps a reduced response rate (Wender et al., 1985; Mattes et al., 1984). Whereas, methylphenidate is at least 70% effective in children, response rates appears to be somewhat lower at 50% in adults. Biederman proposes that these results were not as good because the dose of methylphenidate was in the range of 0.5 to 0.6 mg/kg, which is usually prescribed in children and results in underdosing in adults (Jaffe, 1993/1994).

Dextroamphetamine (Dexedrine)

Since Bradley first gave Benzedrine to a group of retarded, institutionalized children in 1937 and noted behavioral improvement, amphetamines have been given to children with hyperactive behaviors for over 50 years. Their efficacy is well established and ranges from 75 to 96%. Side effects and limitations of treatment response are similar to those of methylphenidate described above. Dextroamphetamine reduces motor activity and decreases symptoms of hyperactivity and impulsiveness. In 1978, Rapoport and associates demonstrated that dextroamphetamine was effective and had both cognitive and behavioral effects even in normal prepubertal boys. In this study, there was a marked decrease in motor activity and reaction time, and improved performance on cognitive tests was reported. A marked behavioral rebound (increased talkativeness, excitability, and apparent euphoria) was observed by parents and teachers starting approximately 5 hours after medication was given, however.

Short and longer-acting forms of dexedrine are available with a new product (Adderol) just becoming available. Adderol is composed of four salts of a single-entity amphetamine and contains both dextro- and levo-amphetamine.

Pemoline (Cylert)

In early studies comparing dextroamphetamine and pemoline, both drugs were found to produce highly significant treatment responses, with dextroamphetamine resulting in a 96% improvement and pemoline a slightly lower one of 77%. While dextroamphetamine showed clear results by the end of 2 weeks, pemoline was slower, but its effects were indistinguishable from those of dextroamphetamine by 8 weeks of treatment (Conners, 1972). However, recent studies of pemoline indicate that with higher doses and more rapid increases, more effective levels may be reached sooner (Pelham et al., 1995).

Long Acting Stimulants

At this time, stimulants not only exist in a standard form but also as a long-acting preparation. A study by Pelham and coworkers (1990) has looked at the relative efficacy of sustained-release methylphenidate, sustained-release dextro-amphetamine, and pemoline. It revealed that these preparations had generally equivalent and beneficial effects and that dexedrine and pemoline tended to produce the most consistent effects, both increasing prosocial and decreasing antisocial behaviors. These medications were all found to have effect within 1 to 2 hours of ingestion, and effects lasted for up to 9 hours. This study also documented that pemoline was found to have effects on the second or third day of treatment, thus contradicting common beliefs that efficacy takes much longer to achieve with this drug (Pelham et al., 1990).

Nonstimulants

While stimulants remain an important part of any treatment program, they may not address all of the symptoms related to ADD and in some cases are clearly not effective. Other medications have been found to be useful in these cases.

Clonidine (Catapres)

Clonidine an alpha2-noradrenergic receptor agonist, has been found to be particularly effective in treating those children who are hyperaroused, overvigilant, and overanxious (Hunt et al., 1990). In addition, studies have found clonidine to be effective in improving behavioral symptoms in 70% of children treated, as measured on parent and teacher rating scales (Hunt et al., 1985). In children with ADD and comorbid tic disorder, clonidine has also been suggested as an alternative pharmacotherapy (Steingard et al., 1993). Tenex (guanfacine) another centrally acting antihypertensive agent, may also be effective in this group and have much less sedation, a common side effect.

Guanfacine (Tenex)

The use of guanfacine (Tenex), an alpha-2-noradrenergic agonist similar to clonidine, has also been studied as an alternative to stimulants because of its longer half-life and decreased side effects. Several studies, the most recent by Hunt and co-workers (1995), indicate that during guanfacine treatment, improvements were noted on the Conners Parent Rating Scale. Mean scores improved significantly, as did Hyperactivity, Inattention, and Immaturity factors. Guanfacine thus appears to be an effective and useful treatment for the treatment of ADD, reducing hyperactive symptomatology and enabling increased attention span with minimal side effects (Hunt et al., 1995).

Tricyclic Antidepressants (Imipramine, Desipramine)

When stimulants do not work or side effects are significant, the tricyclics have proven to be effective alternatives. They may also be effective in children with depression or anxiety occurring concomitantly with ADD or with those who experience adverse side effects (Pliszka, 1987). Huessy and Wright (1970) studied children on tricyclics who were nonresponders to stimulants and found that 67% showed marked improvement on rating scales completed by parents and teachers. In most of the children who improved, one dose in the evening was sufficient to effect change throughout the day, with doses varying from 25 to 125 mg. In a double-blind study comparing the efficacy of imipramine and methylphenidate, Rapoport and associates (1974) found that while both drugs were superior to placebo, all measures favored the stimulant drug for treatment response. Although the tricyclic had some initial effect it seemed to wear off after about 10 weeks. There was only a weak effect for imipramine, displayed on cognitive testing. The mean dose of imipramine in this study was 80 mg, which was somewhat lower than that used in other studies (Rapoport et al., 1974).

Donnelly and colleagues (1986) conducted further studies of the tricyclic desipramine. Hyperactivity/impulsivity ratings and classroom motor activity showed a marked decrease from baseline; cognitive measures, however, did not improve with medication (Donnelly et al., (1986). Similar results were found in several large studies carried out by Biederman and coworkers (1986, 1989a, b), which later looked at the potential cardiovascular side effects and risk of sudden death (Biederman et al., 1993; Biederman, 1991a, b).

Antidepressants

Fluoxetine (Prozac) has been less well studied as an agent for the treatment of ADD. In a preliminary study, Barrickman and coworkers evaluated 19 children and adolescents with ADD treated for six weeks with fluoxetine. Approximately 60% of the subjects were felt to be at least moderately improved by the end of this study and side effects were minimal (Barrickman et al., 1991). While comorbid depressive symptomatology appears to be affected, it is at this time not clear whether symptoms of ADD are improved on this treatment regimen. Studies looking at combined therapy for children with ADD and other comorbid conditions indicate that after inadequate response to methylphenidate alone, treatment with both methylphenidate and fluoxetine reduces depressive symptoms by two-thirds, with a global improvement in functioning by about one-third in these children (Gammon & Brown, 1993). Bupropion (Wellbutrin) is another antide-

pressant that has been proposed as an alternative to stimulants in children (Clay et al., 1988; Casat et al., 1989) and
adults with ADD (Wender & Reimherr, 1990).

MAO Inhibitors

Comparison of dextroamphetamine and MAO inhibitors in
a double-blind crossover study (Zametkin et al., 1985) revealed that the MAO inhibitors had immediate, clinically significant benefits which were almost indistinguishable from
those of dextroamphetamine. These drugs, however, have limited usefulness because of possible side effects and dietary re-
strictions at higher doses.

COMBINED THERAPY

For some patients it is clearly necessary to use a combination
therapy approach to achieve psychopharmacologic management of all of their symptoms. For treatment of adults with
ADD whose symptoms of impulsivity and lack of behavioral
control have been resistant to stimulants alone, a combination of stimulants and beta blockers has been found to be
quite effective. The beta blocker not only enhances the
stimulant's effectiveness but also addresses symptoms of insomnia and impulsiveness (Ratey et al., 1991).

Children with ADD and aggressivity, Oppositional Defiant
Disorder (ODD), Conduct Disorder (CD), and/or tics tend to
respond favorably to a combination of stimulant and clonidine
or stimulant and tricyclic antidepressant. Clonidine and
desipramine, alone or in combination with other medication,
have been recommended for treatment of ADD in children
with Tourette's syndrome. In a recent study (Singer et al.,
1995), improvement with desipramine was noted to be superior to clonidine on all measures, and clinical improvement
did not correlate with blood levels. Clonidine was also not

noted to improve tic severity on any measure (Singer et al., 1995). When depressive symptomatology accompanies ADD, adding an antidepressant to the stimulant medication appears to address the depressive component adequately (Gammon & Brown, 1993). Anxiety-related disorders seen in children with ADD may respond to a tricyclic antidepressant or clonidine in combination with a stimulant or alone. A newer antianxiety medication, buspirone (Buspar), has recently been tried in these situations as well, particularly in adults. Fluoxetine is recommended for outright panic attacks and/or obsessive-compulsive symptomatology as well as for depression.

Tics are seen fairly commonly in children. It has been estimated that anywhere from 3% (Barabas, 1988) to 15% (Bruun, Cohen, & Lecman, 1989) of the population manifest tics at some time (Barabas, 1988). Likewise, Tourette's syndrome is a complex neurobiological disorder seen in 0.3 to 0.5 per 1,000 population (Hyde & Weinberger, 1995). Of males with Tourette's syndrome under 21 years of age, 62% are said to have ADD (Comings & Comings, 1984). Clonidine is an excellent choice for children with Tourette's syndrome; in my practice, I frequently combine low doses of stimulants, once tics are under control with clonidine, with a resultant improvement of ADD-related attentional problems.

SIDE EFFECTS OF THE VARIOUS PHARMACOLOGIC TREATMENTS FOR ADD

While the efficacy of stimulant medication cannot be denied, its use is not without some short-term side effects. The most frequent ones are decreased appetite (anorexia) with subsequent decreased food intake, resulting in possible weight loss and insomnia (Barkley et al., 1990; Barkley, 1977). Both of these effects may be lessened by a decrease in dose or a change in dosage schedule for a brief period. Decreased food intake may be addressed by taking medication after meals and supplementing calories at mealtimes. For many patients, frequent small high-calorie yet nutritious snacks or liquid supplements have be effective in dealing with these problems.

Many individuals with ADD also have significant sleep disturbances including trouble falling asleep, difficulty staying asleep, or trouble waking up in the morning. Many infants and young children with ADD fail to sleep through the night within the expected time frame and may go several years with night waking. Young children may rise early in the morning (5 A.M. to 6 A.M.) and have trouble settling down at night. Older children and adolescents may have difficulty arising in the morning in addition to difficulty falling asleep at night, although no difference in baseline sleep levels have been found (Haig et al., 1974). For those individuals who are overaroused, methylphenidate may actually normalize sleep patterns, allowing patients to settle down better in the evening and arise with less difficulty in the morning. Recent work by Tirosh and coworkers (1993) on the activity levels and effects of methylphenidate on sleep in children with ADD seems to support these clinical observations. Sleep duration for children with ADD which had been longer than that of controls during baseline and placebo phases of the study, were significantly shorter on methylphenidate. There was no significant difference in other sleep indices, thus indicating that treatment with methylphenidate may in fact normalize sleep patterns.

If stimulants, conversely, worsen the insomnia found in ADD in some individuals, this problem can be addressed by decreasing caffeine intake during the day, increasing regular exercise, and making sure that the last dose of stimulant medication has worn off prior to bedtime. Clonidine may also be added to the medication regime for cases where inability to sleep is due to significant overarousal.

The frequency of side effects of methylphenidate in children were quite thoroughly investigated by Barkley and colleagues (1990) in their triple-blind placebo-controlled crossover study of the effects of two doses of methylphenidate and placebo. A total of 83 children were studied and ratings of side effects were obtained weekly from parents and teachers. Only 3 children (3.6%) had side effects that were severe enough to discontinue the medication. Decreased appetite, insomnia, stomachaches, and headaches were the only symptoms that significantly increased in frequency and severity, according to parent reports. Teacher ratings reported little change in these symptoms during the study period. At the higher dose level, they did, however, report a decrease in staring, sadness, and anxiety. A high frequency of these same symptoms had been seen during the placebo period (Barkley et al., 1990).

In 1972, Safer and associates reported, in the *New England Journal of Medicine*, that children taking dextroamphetamine or methylphenidate experienced a suppression in weight gain. Children who had depression of growth in weight also had proportional depression of growth in height. Suppression of weight gain, although not dose-related, appeared to be more significant for dextroamphetamine than methylphenidate. Tolerance developed to the weight suppression effects of dextroamphetamine but not to inhibition of height growth. Daily doses of methylphenidate of 20 mg did not appear to inhibit weight gain (Safer et al., 1972; Safer & Allen, 1973). Further studies of methylphenidate indicated that an adverse effect on both height and weight seen during the first year of treatment was not seen in subsequent years and that the first-year height deficit is offset by a greater-than-expected growth rate in the second year. These side effects were not seen to correlate with dosage. Height deficits were not related to total dose or summer drug holidays, but weight deficits did appear to be related to these factors (Satterfield et al., 1979).

In addition, studies with adolescents have found no significant decreases in height or weight, suggesting that these findings are applicable only to prepubertal children (Vincent et al., 1990). While this particular study was relatively short (6 to 12 months; mean, 7.3 months), other follow-up studies in adults who received treatment as children and adolescents do not indicate any ultimate growth suppression. Long-term studies of young adults treated with methylphenidate found no significant difference in ultimate height between treated and control subjects. Both groups were at the national norms, with no compromise seen in the treated group even if there was an adverse effect on growth rate during active treatment (Klein & Mannuzza, 1988).

Rebound weight gain was noted when medication was discontinued. In one study, discontinuation of stimulant treatment from June to September resulted in a growth rebound that was 15 to 68% above the age-expected rate (Safer et al., 1975). These findings were confirmed by the 1976 study by Gross of the growth of children taking methylphenidate, dextroamphetamine, or imipramine/ desipramine. Here again there was initially some diminution in weight but not in height. Subsequent growth was found to be greater than predicted, particularly for those children whose medication was stopped prior to completion of the study. Again, no correlations were found between dosage levels and changes in height or weight percentiles; and any slowing of growth which occurred initially appeared to be compensated for as time went on (Gross, 1976).

Higher doses of methylphenidate than those used in the above studies did appear to influence growth in children taking methylphenidate at doses of up to 80 mg/day. In a study of 86 hyperactive children conducted by Mattes and Gittelman (1983), a significant decrease in weight percentiles occurred, with a decrease in height percentiles noted after the first year of treatment at a mean dose of 40 mg/day (Mattes & Gittleman, 1983).

In another study using high doses of methylphenidate, a variance from predicted height and weight was noted at adolescence, especially when there was significant early weight and appetite suppression (Loney et al., 1981). These results do suggest that children on long-term stimulant therapy, especially those on higher doses, need to be monitored closely for effects on growth in both height and weight in adolescence and young adulthood.

It has been postulated that the growth suppression seen during stimulant treatment may be the direct result of neuroendocrine growth regulation. The stimulant drugs methylphenidate and dextroamphetamine were found to have an acute and probably long-term effects on growth hormone homeostasis and to cause a release in growth hormone similar to that seen during L-dopa stimulation testing (Aarskog et al., 1977). In other studies, prolactin levels were noted to fall after 6 months of treatment with dextroamphetamine (Puig-Antich et al., 1978; Greenhill et al., 1981), but there were no noticeable effects on growth hormone (Greenhill et al., 1981). No effects on prolactin but slight increases in sleep-related growth hormone levels with prolonged treatment with methylphenidate were also noted (Greenhill et al., 1984), with significant increases in growth hormone noted to be dose-related in hyperactive children (Gualtieri et al., 1981).

Hunt and colleagues studied the effects of methylphenidate on growth hormone by using clonidine to stimulate growth hormone release. During treatment with methylphenidate, a significant decrease in response to clonidine was noted from pretreatment levels. In addition, growth hormone values in response to clonidine returned to pretreatment levels as soon as 1 day after discontinuing the methylphenidate (Hunt et al., 1984).

A decrease in height velocity was seen in children receiving pemoline therapy. This effect likewise appears to be dose-related, as children receiving less than a median dose of 3.72 mg/kg grew 4 cm/year or more, while patients receiving more than this dose grew at a slower rate (Dickinson et al., 1979). Decrease in weight appears to be limited to the initial therapy period (12 months) with subsequent measure for up to 4 years not revealing any significant differences. A decrease in height velocity was noted for the first 18 months; this also normal-ized after that period (Friedmann et al., 1981). Body weight and appetite do not seem to be as affected by pemoline, but liver dysfunction and more significant insomnia than with the other stimulants has been reported. A review of reported cases of hepatotoxicity indicated that this was occurring at doses of less than 100 mg/day and after approximately 10 to 12 months of therapy, but that these findings were extremely variable (Nehra et al., 1990). Therefore it is recommended that liver functions be monitored regularly (approximately every 3 months) for children on this preparation.

While slight but significant weight deficits have been found for children treated with desipramine, no significant changes in height were seen. Both of these observed effects were less than those seen with methylphenidate (Quinn & Rapoport, 1975; Spencer et al., 1992). Of greater concern, however, are the rare incidences of sudden deaths seen in children on tricyclic antidepressants (Popper & Elliott, 1990). Biederman (1991a, b) reports that 35% of nearly 200 children taking desipramine developed sinus tachycardia, 0.5% had atrioventricular block, and 3% had complete right bundle branch block. While there is insufficient evidence to link the deaths of these children to treatment with desipramine, certain precautions should be taken in prescribing this class of drugs for children (Elliott & Popper, 1990/1991). Guidelines for use of tricyclics in children under the age of 12 years include obtaining an electrocardiogram (ECG) prior to initiation of medication, with subsequent ECGs as dosage is raised to therapeutic levels. Subsequently, routine monitoring while patients are on maintenance therapy or whenever cardiac symptoms occur is required. Blood levels should also be monitored to keep them within the therapeutic range. A dose reduction or discontinuation of drug is recommended if the PR interval exceeds or is equal to 0.21 seconds or if the QRS widens more that 30% over baseline (Puig-Antich et al., 1987; Ryan, 1990).

Very rare cases of hypersensitivity to methylphenidate and dextroamphetamine have been reported. Most reports of allergic reactions involve the skin; i.e., there may be rashes, photosensitivity, or urticaria (hives) (Sverd et al., 1977). Another rare side effect (probably less than 1%) may be in the induction of psychosis and/or hallucinations (Oettinger & Majovski, 1976; Lucas & Weiss, 1971; Young, 1981). Immediate discontinuation of the stimulant is recommended in such cases. Contrary to prior belief, it has recently been documented that methylphenidate does not lower the seizure threshold or cause an increase in seizures (McBridge et al., 1986; Feldman et al., 1989).

More commonly, one can see a tolerance to a particular stimulant develop after several years of treatment. If this occurs, switching to another stimulant usually proves an effective remedy. The rebound phenomenon upon discontinuation of stimulant medication may be seen and may include a worsening of hyperactive symptoms, headache, and irritability. These behaviors may also be seen to a lesser degree as the dose of stimulant medication is wearing off. In a recent study, about one-third of the sample treated with multiple doses of methylphenidate experienced a rebound behavioral effect but none to the extent that required changes in their medication (Johnston et al., 1988). Overlapping of doses or a change to the long-acting preparation may alleviate this phenomenon.

Clinical evidence has supported the observation that stimulant medication increases tics in 25 to 50% of patients with Tourette's syndrome (Golden, 1988), but there is considerable controversy regarding their actually precipitating the disorder. Some studies (Comings & Comings, 1984) have even suggested that Tourette's syndrome and ADD are manifestations of the same gene and that onset of the tics of Tourette's syndrome is prolonged in those individuals who have been treated with stimulants for their ADD. Similar problems of increasing tic behavior have been reported for imipramine (Price et al., 1986) but not desipramine (Hoge & Biederman, 1986; Singer et al., 1995). Abnormal involuntary movements have also been noted in children receiving pemoline (Sallee et al., 1989).

CONCLUSION

As we have seen, ADD is a complex disorder and single-modality treatment is generally not effective in dealing with the wide range of symptoms and the problems they create. While effective in treating some symptoms in 75 to 85% of patients with ADD, medication alone is not the answer. A therapy component that includes both counseling and training in self-control (behavior) and cognitive strategies is also essential. Parent education, behavior management training, and family-based treatment are also integral components of a multimodal program.

It is critical to treat the child with ADD as part of a family, thereby positively affecting both parental attitudes and parent–child interactions. After all, it is "through participation in education and support groups and training in behavior-management techniques, [that] families can begin to feel empowered in that they are the interventions that produce therapeutic changes" (Coker & Thyer, 1990, p. 281).

For adults with ADD, medication, increased structure and organization, counseling, "coaching," and support groups are all essential elements of an effective treatment program. Outcomes can be improved, and with adaptations and accommodations, the individuals with ADD can direct their own lives toward achievable, realistic goals. With the support of family, significant others, and employers, the adults with ADD who are willing to advocate for themselves can achieve success.

For those desiring more in-depth coverage of the above therapies, including educational materials for the treatment of ADD, the following resources may prove useful:

RESOURCES FOR PROFESSIONALS

Managing Attention Deficit Disorders in Children: A Guide for Practitioners by Sam Goldstein and Michael Goldstein, 1990, New York: Wiley. 449 pages, $60.00.

Managing Attention Disorders and Learning Disabilities in Late Adolescents and Adults: A Guide for Practitioners by Sam Goldstein and Michael Goldstein, 1996, New York: Wiley. 450 pages, $45.00.

Cognitive-Behavioral Therapy with ADHD Children: Child, Family, and School Interventions by Lauren Braswell and Michael Bloomquist, 1991, New York: Guilford Press. 391 pages, $40.00.

Ritalin: Theory and Patient Management by Laurence Greenhill and Betty Osman (Eds.), 1991, Larchmont, NY: Mary Ann Liebert. 320 pages, $95.00.

Medications for Attention Disorders (ADHD/ADD) and Related Medical Problems by Edna Copeland, Atlanta, GA: SPI Press. 420 pages, $35.00.

Textbook of Pharmacotherapy for Child and Adolescent Psychiatric Disorders by David Resenberg, John Holttum, and Samuel Gershon, 1994, New York: Brunner/Mazel, 570 pages, $65.00

The Attending Physician Attention Deficit Disorder: A Guide for Pediatrician and Family Physicians by Stephen Copps, 1992, Atlanta, GA: SPI Press. 180 pages, $30.00.

A Primary Care Physician's Desk Reference to the Medical and Medication Management of Attention Deficit Hyperactivity Disorder by Keith Baurer, 157 pages.

Attention Deficit Hyperactivity Disorder: A Clinical Guide to Diagnosis and Treatment by Larry Silver, 1991, Washington, DC: American Psychiatric Press. 164 pages.

Feeding the Brain: How Foods Affect Children by C. Keith Conners, 1989, New York: Plenum. 277 pages, $24.00.

VIDEOS

Medication for Attention Deficit Disorder: All You Need to Know by Thomas Phelan and Jonathan Bloombery.

RESOURCES FOR CHILDREN

Otto Learns About His Medicine, Revised Edition by Michael Gavin, 1995, New York: Magination Press. 32 pages, $11.95.

Putting on the Brakes: Young People's Guide to Understanding Attention Deficit Hyperactivity Disorder by Patricia Quinn and Judith Stern, 1991, New York: Magination Press. 64 pages, $9.95.

Putting on the Brakes Activity Book by Patricia Quinn and Judith Stern, 1993, New York: Magination Press. 88 pages, $14.95.

REFERENCES

Aarskog, D., Fevang, F. O., Klove, H., Stoa, K. F., & Thorsen, T. (1977). The effect of the stimulant drugs, dextroamphetamine, and methylphenidate on secretion of growth hormone in hyperactive children. *Journal of Pediatrics, 90*, 136–139.

Abikoff, H. (1991). Cognitive training in ADHD children: Less to it than meets the eye. *Journal of Learning Disabilities, 24*, 205–209.

Abikoff, H., & Gittleman, R. (1985). Hyperactive children maintained on stimulants: Is cognitive training a useful adjunct? *Archives of General Psychiatry, 42*, 953–961.

Adams, W. (1982). Effect of methylphenidate on thought processing time in children. *Journal of Developmental and Behavioral Pediatrics, 3*, 133–135.

Anastopoulos, A. D., DuPaul, G. J., & Barkley, R. A. (1991). Stimulant medication and parent training therapies for attention deficit-hyperactivity disorder. *Journal of Learning Disabilities, 24*, 210–218.

Backman, J., & Firestone, P. (1979). A review of psychopharmacological and behavioral approaches to the treatment of hyperactive children. *American Journal of Orthopsychiatry, 49*, 500–504.

Barabas, G. (1988). Tourette's syndrome: An overview. *Pediatric Annals, 17*, 391–393.

Baren, M. (1994). Managing ADHD. *Contemporary Pediatrics, 11*, 29–48.

Barkley, R. A. (1977). The effects of methylphenidate on various types of activity level and attention in hyperkinetic children. *Journal of Abnormal Child Psychology, 5*, 351–369.

Barkley, R. A. (1979). Using stimulant drugs in the classroom. *School Psychology Digest, 8*, 412–425.

Barkley, R. A. (1985). The social behavior of hyperactive children: Developmental changes, drug effects, and situational variation. In R. McMahon & R. Peters (Eds.), *Childhood disorders.* New York: Brunner/Mazel.

Barkley, R. A. (1990). *Attention deficit hyperactivity disorder: A handbook for diagnosis and treatment.* New York: Guilford.

Barkley, R. A., Copeland, A. P., & Sivage, C. (1980). A self-control classroom for hyperactive children. *Journal of Autism and Developmental Disorders, 10*, 75–89.

Barkley, R. A., & Cunningham, C. D. (1978). Do stimulant drugs improve the academic performance of hyperkinetic children?: A review of outcome research. *Clinical Pediatrics, 17*, 85–92.

Barkley, R. A., & Cunningham, C. E. (1979a). Stimulant drugs and activity level in hyperactive children. *American Journal of Orthopsychiatry, 49*, 491–499.

Barkley, R. A., & Cunningham, C. E. (1979b). The effects of methylphenidate on the mother–child interactions of hyperactive children. *Archives of General Psychiatry, 36*, 201–208.

Barkley, R. A., & Cunningham, C. E. (1980). The parent–child interactions of hyperactive children and their modification by stimulant drugs. In R. M. Knights & D. J. Bakker (Eds.), *Treatment of hyperactive and learning disordered children.* Baltimore: University Press.

Barkley, R. A., DuPaul, G. J., & McMurray, M. B. (1991). Attention deficit disorder with and without hyperactivity: Clinical response to three dose levels of methylphenidate. *Pediatrics, 87*, 519–531.

Barkley, R. A., Karlsson, J., Pollard, S., & Murphy, J. V. (1985). Developmental changes in the mother–child interactions of hyperactive boys: Effects of two dose levels of Ritalin. *Journal of Child Psychology and Psychiatry, 26*, 705–715.

Barkley, R. A., McMurray, M. B., Edelbrock, C. S., & Robbins, K. (1989). The response of aggressive and nonaggressive ADHD children to two doses of methylphenidate. *Journal of the American Academy of Child and Adolescent Psychiatry, 28,* 873–881.

Barkley, R. A., McMurray, M. B., Edelbrock, C. S., & Robbins, K. (1990). Side effects of methylphenidate in children with attention deficit hyperactivity disorder: A systemic, placebo-controlled evaluation. *Pediatrics, 86,* 184–192.

Barrickman, L., Noyes, R., Kuperman, S., Schumacher, E., & Verda, M. (1991). Treatment of ADHD with fluoxetine: A preliminary trial. *Journal of the American Academy of Child and Adolescent Psychiatry, 30,* 762–767.

Biederman, J. (1991a). Sudden death in children treated with a tricylic antidepressant. *Journal of the American Academy of Child and Adolescent Psychiatry, 30,* 495–498.

Biederman, J. (1991b). Sudden death in children treated with a tricyclic antidepressant: A commentary. *Biological and Therapeutic Psychiatry Newsletter, 14,* 1–4.

Biederman, J., Baldessarini, R. J., Goldblatt, A., et al. (1993). A naturalistic study of 24-hour electrocardiographic recordings and echocardiographic findings in children and adolescents treated with desipramine. *Journal of the American Academy of Child and Adolescent Psychiatry, 32,* 805–813.

Biederman, J., Baldessarini, R. J., Wright, V., et al. (1989a). A double-blind placebo controlled study of desipramine in the treatment of ADD, I: Efficacy. *Journal of the American Academy of Child and Adolescent Psychiatry, 28,* 777–784.

Biederman, J., Baldessarini, R. J., Wright, V., et al. (1989b). A double-blind placebo controlled study of desipramine in the treatment of ADD, II: Serum drug levels and cardiovascular findings. *Journal of the American Academy of Child and Adolescent Psychiatry, 28,* 903–911.

Biederman, J., Baldessarini, R. J., Wright, B. A., Keenan, K., & Faraone, S. (1993). A double-blind placebo controlled study of desipramine in the treatment of ADD, III: Lack of impact of comorbidity and family history factors on clinical response. *Journal of the American Academy of Child and Adolescent Psychiatry, 32,* 199–204.

Biederman, J., Gastfriend, D. R., & Jellinek, M. S. (1986). Desipramine in the treatment of children with attention deficit disorder. *Journal of Clinical Psychopharmacology, 6,* 359–363.

Brown, R. T., & Sexson, S. B. (1988). A controlled trial of methylphenidate in black adolescents. *Clinical Pediatrics, 27,* 74–81.

Bruun, R. D., Cohen, D. J., & Leckman, J. F. (1989). *Guide to the diagnosis and treatment of Tourette syndrome.* Bayside, NY: Tourette Syndrome Association.

Casat, C. D., Pleasants, D. Z., & Schroeder, D. H. (1989). Buproprion in children with attention deficit disorder. *Psychopharmacology Bulletin, 25,* 198–201.

Clay, T. H., Gaultieri, C. T., & Evans, R. W. (1988). Clinical and neuropsychological effects of the novel antidepressant buproprion. *Psychopharmacology Bulletin, 24,* 143–148.

Coker, K. H., & Thyer, B. A. (1990). School- and family-based treatment of children with attention-deficit hyperactivity disorder. *Families in Society: The Journal of Contemporary Human Services,* May, 281.

Comings, D. E., & Comings, B. G. (1984). Tourette's syndrome and attention deficit disorder with hyperactivity: Are they genetically related? *Journal of the American Academy of Child Psychiatry, 23,* 138–146.

Conners, C. K. (1972). Symposium: Behavior modification by drugs, II: Psychological effects of stimulant drugs in children with minimal brain dysfunction. *Pediatrics, 49,* 702–708.

Culbert, T. P., Banez, G. A., & Reiff, M. I. (1994). Children who have attentional disorders: Interventions. *Pediatrics in Review, 15,* 5–15.

Cunningham, C. E., & Barkley, R. A. (1978). The effects of methylphenidate on the mother–child interactions of hyperactive identical twins. *Developmental Medicine and Child Neurology, 20,* 634–642.

Dickinson, L. C., Lee, J., Ringdahl, I. C., Schedewie, H. K., et al. (1979). Impaired growth in hyperkinetic children receiving pemoline. *Journal of Pediatrics, 94,* 538–541.

Donnelly, M., Zametkin, A. J., Rapoport, J. L., et al. (1986). Treatment of childhood hyperactivity with desipramine: Plasma drug concentration, cardiovascular effects, plasma and urinary catecholamine levels, and clinical response. *Clinical Pharmacology and Therapeutics, 39,* 72–81.

Douglas, V. (1975). Are drugs enough to treat or train the hyperactive child? *International Journal of Mental Health, 5,* 199–212.

Dulcan, M. K. (1985). The psychopharmacologic treatment of children and adolescents with attention deficit disorder. *Psychiatric Annals, 15,* 69–87.

Dulcan, M. K. (1990). Using psychostimulants to treat behavioral disorders of children and adolescents. *Journal of Child and Adolescent Psychopharmacology, 1,* 7–20.

DuPaul, G. J., & Rapport, M. D. (1993). Does methylphenidate normalize the classroom performance of children with attention deficit disorder? *Journal of the American Academy of Child and Adolescent Psychiatry, 32,* 190–198.

Elliott, G. R., & Popper, C. W. (1990/1991). Tricyclic antidepressants: The QT interval and other cardiovascular parameters. *Journal of Child and Adolescent Psychopharmacology, 1,* 187–189.

Famularo, R., & Fenton, T. (1987). The effect of methylphenidate on school grades in children with attention deficit disorder without hyperactivity: A preliminary report. *Journal of Clinical Psychiatry, 48,* 112–114.

Feldman, H., Crumrine, P., Handen, B. L., et al. (1989). Methylphenidate in children with seizures and attention deficit disorder. *American Journal of Diseases in Children, 143,* 1081–1086.

Friedmann, N., Thomas, J., Carr, R., et al. (1981). Effect on growth in pemoline-treated children with attention deficit disorder. *American Journal of Diseases in Children, 135,* 329–332.

Funk, J. B., Chessare, J. B., Weaver, M. T., & Exley, A. R. (1993). Attention deficit hyperactivity disorder, creativity, and the effects of methylphenidate. *Pediatrics, 91,* 816–819.

Gammon, G. D., & Brown, T. E. (1993). Fluoxetine and methylphenidate in combination for treatment of attention deficit disorder and comorbid depressive disorder. *Journal of Child and Adolescent Psychopharmacology, 3,* 1–10.

Gittleman, R. (1980). Drug treatment of child psychiatric disorders. In D. F. Klein, R. Gittleman, F. Quitkin, & A. Rifken (Eds.), *Diagnosis and treatment of psychiatric disorders* (2nd ed.) (pp. 590–696). Baltimore: Williams & Wilkins.

Goff, G., & Demetral, D. (1983). A home-based program to eliminate aggression in the classroom. *Social Work in Education, 5,* 5–14.

Golden, G. S. (1988). The relationship between stimulant medication and tics. *Pediatric Annals, 17,* 405–408.

Goldstein, S., & Goldstein, M. (1990). *Managing attention disorders in children: A guide for practitioners.* New York: Wiley.

Greenhill, L. L., Puig-Antich, J., Chambers, W., et al. (1981). Growth hormone, prolactin, and growth responses in hyperkinetic males treated with d-amphetamine. *Journal of the American Academy of Child Psychiatry, 20,* 84–103.

Greenhill, L., Puig-Antich, J., Novacenko, H., et al. (1984). Prolactin, growth hormone and growth responses in boys with attention deficit disorder and hyperactivity treated with methylphenidate. *Journal of the American Academy of Child Psychiatry, 23,* 58–67.

Gross, M. D. (1976). Growth of hyperkinetic children taking methylphenidate, dextroamphetamine, or imipramine/desipramine. *Pediatrics, 58,* 423–431.

Gualtieri, C. T., Kanoy, R., Hawk, B., et al. (1981). Growth hormone and prolactin secretion in adults and hyperactive children: Relation to methylphenidate serum levels. *Psychoneuroendocrinology, 6,* 331–339.

Haig, J. R., Schraeder, C. S., & Schroeder, S. R. (1994). Effects of methylphenidate on hyperactive children's sleep. *Psychopharmacology, 37,* 185–188.

Hoge, S. K., & Biederman, J. (1986). A case of Tourette's syndrome with symptoms of attention deficit disorder treated with desipramine. *Journal of Clinical Psychiatry, 47,* 478–479.

Horn, W., Ialongo, N., Popovich, S., & Peradotto, D. (1987). Behavioral parent training and cognitive-behavioral self-control therapy with ADHD children: Comparative and combined effects. *Journal of Clinical Child Psychiatry, 16,* 57–68.

Huessy, H. R., & Wright, A. L. (1970). The use of imipramine in children's behavior disorders. *International Journal of Child Psychology, 37,* 194–199.

Hunt, R. D., Arnstein, A. F., & Asbell, M. D. (1995). An open trial of guanfacine in the treatment of attention deficit hyperactivity disorder. *Journal of the American Academy of Child and Adolescent Psychiatry, 34,* 50–54.

Hunt, R. D., Capper, L., & O'Connell, P. (1990). Clonidine in child and adolescent psychiatry. *Journal of Child and Adolescent Psychopharmacology, 1,* 87–102.

Hunt, R. D., Cohen, D. J., Anderson, G., et al. (1984). Possible change in noradrenergic receptor sensitivity following methylphenidate treatment: Growth hormone and MHPG response to clonidine challenge in children with attention deficit disorders and hyperactivity. *Life Science, 35,* 885–897.

Hunt, R. D., Minderaa, R. B., & Cohen, D. J. (1985). Clonidine benefits children with attention deficit disorder and hyperactivity: Report of a double-blind placebo-crossover therapeutic trial. *Journal of the American Academy of Child Psychiatry, 24,* 617–629.

Hyde, T. M., & Weinberger, D. R. (1995). Tourette's syndrome: A model neuropsychiatric disorder. *Journal of the American Medical Association, 273,* 498–501.

Ialongo, N. S., Horn, W. F., Pascoe, J. M., et al. (1993). The effects of a multimodal intervention with attention-deficit hyperactivity disorder children: A 9-month follow-up. *Journal of the American Academy of Child and Adolescent Psychiatry, 32,* 182–189.

Ingersoll, B. D., & Goldstein, S. (1993). *Attention deficit disorder and learning disabilities: Realities, myths and controversial treatments.* New York: Doubleday.

Jaffe, P. (Ed.). (1993/1994). Ritalin and adults: Too late or too little? *ADDendum,* Issue 14–15, 1, 14.

Johnston, C., Pelham, W. E., Hoza, J., & Sturges, J. (1988). Psychostimulant rebound in attention deficit disordered boys. *Journal of the American Academy of Child and Adolescent Psychiatry, 27,* 806–810.

Keith, R. W., & Engineer, P. (1991). Effects of methylphenidate on the auditory processing abilities of children with attention deficit-hyperactivity disorder. *Journal of Learning Disabilities, 24,* 630–636.

Klein, R. G., & Mannuzza, S. (1988). Hyperactive boys almost grown up. *Archives of General Psychiatry, 45,* 1131–1134.

Liu, C., Robin, A. L., Brenner, S., & Eastman, J. (1991). Social acceptability of methylphenidate and behavior modification for treating attention deficit hyperactivity disorder. *Pediatrics, 88,* 560–565.

Loney, J., Weissenburger, F. E., Woolson, R. F., & Lichty, E. C.

(1979). Comparing psychological and pharmacological treatments for hyperkinetic boys and their classmates. *Journal of Abnormal Child Psychology, 7*, 133–143.

Loney, J., Whaley-Klahn, M. A., Ponto, L. B., & Adney, K. (1981). Predictors of adolescent height and weight in hyperkinetic boys treated with methylphenidate. *Psychopharmacology Bulletin, 17*, 132–134.

Lucas, A. R., & Weiss, M. (1971). Methylphenidate hallucinosis. *Journal of the American Medical Association, 217*, 1079–1081.

Mattes, J. A., Boswell, L., & Oliver, H. (1984). Methylphenidate effects on symptoms of attention deficit disorder in adults. *Archives of General Psychiatry, 41*, 1059–1063.

Mattes, J. A., & Gittelman, R. (1983). Growth of hyperactive children on maintenance regimen of methylphenidate. *Archives of General Psychiatry, 40*, 317–321.

McBridge, M. C., Wang, D. D., & Torres, C. F. (1986). Methylphenidate in therapeutic doses does not lower seizure threshold. *Annals of Neurology, 20*, 428.

Nehra, A., Mullick, F., Ishak, K. G., & Zimmerman, H. J. (1990). Pemoline-associated hepatic injury. *Gastroenterology, 99*, 1517–1519.

Oettinger, L., & Majovski, L. V. (1976). Methylphenidate: A review. *Southern Medical Journal, 69*, 161–163.

Pelham, W. E. (1989). Behavior therapy, behavioral assessment and psychostimulant medication in the treatment of attention deficit disorders: An interactive approach. In L. Bloomingdale & J. Swanson (Eds.), *Attention deficit disorder: Current concepts and emerging trends in attentional and behavioral disorders of childhood.* Oxford, England: Pergamon Press.

Pelham, W., Greenslade, K., Vodde-Hamilton, M., et al. (1990). Relative efficacy of long-acting stimulants on children with attention deficit hyperactivity disorder: A comparison of standard methylphenidate, sustained-release methylphenidate, sustained-release dextroamphetamine, and pemoline. *Pediatrics, 86*, 226–237.

Pelham, W. E., Schnedler, R. W., Bologna, N. C., & Contreras, J. A. (1980). Behavioral and stimulant treatment of hyperactive children: A therapy study with methylphenidate probes in a within-subject design. *Journal of Applied Behavior Analysis, 13*, 221–236.

Pelham, W. E., Swanson, J. M., Furman, M. B., & Schwindt, H. (1995). Pemoline effect on children with ADHD: A time response by dose-response analysis on classroom measures. *Journal of the American Academy of Child and Adolescent Psychiatry, 34,* 1504–1513.

Pelham, W., Walker, J., & Milich, R. (1986). Effects of continuous and partial reinforcement and methylphenidate on learning in children with attention deficit disorder. *Journal of Abnormal Psychology, 95,* 319–325.

Pisterman, S., McGrath, P., Firestone, P., & Goodman, J. T. (1988). Outcome of parent-meditated treatment of preschoolers with attention deficit disorder with hyperactivity. *Journal of Consulting and Clinical Psychology, 57,* 636–643.

Pliszka, S. R. (1987). Tricyclic antidepressants in the treatment of children with attention deficit disorder. *Journal of the Academy of Child and Adolescent Psychiatry, 26,* 127–132.

Popper, C. W., & Elliott, G. R. (1990). Sudden death and tricyclic antidepressants: Clinical considerations for children. *Journal of Child and Adolescent Psychopharmacology, 1,* 125–132.

Price, R. A., Leckman, J. F., Pauls, D. L., et al. (1986). Gilles de la Tourette's syndrome: Tics and central nervous system stimulants in twins and non-twins. *Neurology, 36,* 232–237.

Puig-Antich, J., Greenhill, L. L., Sassin, J., & Sachar, E. (1978). Growth hormone, prolactin and cortisol responses and growth patterns in hyperkinetic children treated with dextroamphetamine. *Journal of the American Academy of Child Psychiatry, 17,* 457–475.

Puig-Antich, J., Perel, J. M., Lupatkin, W., et al. (1987). Imipramine in prepubertal major depressive disorders. *Archives of General Psychiatry, 44,* 81–89.

Quinn, P. O., & Rapoport, J. L. (1975). One year follow-up of hyperactive boys treated with imipramine or methylphenidate. *American Journal of Psychiatry, 132,* 241–245.

Rapoport, J. L., Buchsbaum, M. S., Zahn, T. P., et al. (1978). Dextroamphetamine: Cognitive and behavioral effects in normal prepubertal boys. *Science, 199,* 560–563.

Rapoport, J. L., Quinn, P. O., Bradbard, G., et al. (1974). Imipramine and methylphenidate treatments of hyperactive boys. *Archives of General Psychiatry, 30,* 789–793.

Ratey, J. J., Greenberg, M. S., & Lindem, K. J. (1991).Combination of treatments for attention deficit hyperactivity disorder in adults. *The Journal of Nervous and Mental Disease, 179,* 699–701.

Reid, M. K., & Borkowski, J. G. (1987). Causal attributions of hyperactive children: Implications for teaching strategies and self-control. *Journal of Educational Psychology, 79,* 296–307.

Roche, A. F., Lipman, R. S., Ovreall, J. E., & Hung, W. (1979). The effects of stimulant medication on the growth of hyperkinetic children. *Pediatrics, 63,* 847–850.

Ryan, N. D. (1990). Heterocyclic antidepressants in children and adolescents. *Journal of Child and Adolescent Psychopharmacology, 1,* 21–31.

Safer, D. J., & Allen, R. P. (1973). Factors influencing the suppressant effects of two stimulant drugs on the growth of hyperactive children. *Pediatrics, 51,* 660–667.

Safer, D. J., Allen, R. P., & Barr, E. (1972). Depression of growth in hyperactive children on stimulant drugs. *New England Journal of Medicine, 287,* 217–220.

Safer, D. J., Allen, R. P., & Barr, E. (1975). Growth rebound after termination of stimulant drugs. *Journal of Pediatrics, 86,* 113–116.

Safer, D., & Krager, J. (1994). The increased rate of stimulant treatment for hyperactive/inattentive students in secondary schools. *Pediatrics, 94,* 462–465.

Sallee, F., Stiller, R., Perel, J., & Everett, G. (1989). Pemoline-induced abnormal involuntary movements. *Journal of Clinical Psychopharmacology, 9,* 125–129.

Satterfield, J. H., Cantwell, D. P., Schill, A., & Blaschke, T. (1979). Growth of hyperactive children treated with methylphenidate. *Archives of General Psychiatry, 36,* 212–217.

Singer, H. S., Brown, J., Quaskey, S., et al. (1995). The treatment of attention-deficit hyperactivity disorder in Tourette's syndrome: A double-blind placebo-controlled study with clonidine and desipramine. *Pediatrics, 95,* 74–81.

Spencer, T., Biederman, J., Wright, V., & Danon, M. (1992). Growth deficits in children treated with desipramine: A controlled study. *Journal of the American Academy of Child and Adolescent Psychiatry. 31,* 235–243.

Sprague, R. L., & Sleator, E. K. (1977). Methylphenidate in hyperkinetic children: Differences in dose effects on learning and social behavior. *Science, 198,* 1274.

Steingard, R., Biederman, J., Spencer, T., Wilens, T., & Gonzalez, A. (1993). Comparison of clonidine response in the treatment of attention deficit hyperactivity disorder with and without comorbid tic disorders, *Journal of the American Academy of Child Adolescent Psychiatry, 32,* 350–353.

Sverd, J., Hurwic, M. J., David, O., & Winsberg, B. G. (1977). Hypersensitivity to methylphenidate and dextroamphetamine: A report of two cases. *Pediatrics, 59,* 115–117.

Swanson, J. M., Cantwell, D., Lerner, M., et al. (1991). Effects of stimulant medication on learning in children with ADHD. *Journal of Learning Disabilities, 24,* 219–230.

Tirosh, E., Sadeh, A., Munvez, R., & Lavie, P. (1993). Effects of methylphenidate on sleep in children with attention-deficit hyperactivity disorder. *American Journal of Diseases in Children, 147,* 1313–1315.

Ullmann, R. K., & Sleator, E. K. (1985). Attention deficit disorder children with or without hyperactivity. *Clinical Pediatrics, 24,* 547–551.

Vincent, J., Varley, C., & Leger, P. (1990). Effects of methylphenidate on early adolescent growth. *American Journal of Psychiatry, 147,* 501–502.

Wender, P. H., & Reimherr, F. W. (1990). Buproprion treatment of attention deficit hyperactivity disorder in adults. *American Journal of Psychiatry, 147,* 1018–1020.

Wender, P. H., Reimherr, F. W., Wood, D. R., & Ward, M. (1985). A controlled study of methylphenidate in the treatment of attention deficit, residual type in adults. *American Journal of Psychiatry, 142,* 547–552.

Whitehouse, D., Shah, U., & Palmer, F. B. (1980). Comparison of sustained-release and standard methylphenidate in the treatment of minimal brain dysfunction. *Journal of Clinical Psychiatry, 41,* 282–285.

Wilens, T. E., & Biederman, J. (1992). The stimulants. *Pediatric Psychopharmacology, 15,* 191–222.

Young, J. G. (1981). Methylphenidate-induced hallucinosis: Case histories and possible mechanisms of action. *Developmental and Behavioral Pediatrics, 2,* 35–38.

Zametkin, A., Rapoport, J. L., Murphy, D. L., et al. (1985). Treatment of hyperactive children with monoamine oxidase inhibitors. *Archives of General Psychiatry, 42,* 962–966.

Chapter 9

ADD AND THE LAW

What does a practitioner need to know in order to help the patient/client gain access to services to which they are entitled? Knowledge of the law may not always make the road smoother, but it definitely provides ammunition for the fight. The information provided in this chapter is not all-inclusive and certainly should not be considered legal advice to be used in individual cases, but it may serve to make you more familiar with the individual's rights and the laws from which they stem.

ADD is considered a disability under federal laws when it substantially limits a major life activity such as learning or working. Individuals with disabilities are covered by these laws to avoid discrimination in education or employment. Some laws may apply in special circumstances and not others. For example, a student with ADD may be protected by the Individuals with Disabilities Act (IDEA) and/or Section 504 of the Rehabilitation Act (RA) at the elementary or high school level, but at the postsecondary level only the (RA) may apply.

Children with ADD are guaranteed free and appropriate public education by three federal laws. These are the Individuals with Disabilities Education Act of 1990 (IDEA), Section 504 of the Rehabilitation Act of 1973 (RA), and the Americans with Disabilities Act of 1990 (ADA).

THE INDIVIDUALS WITH DISABILITIES EDUCATION ACT (IDEA)

SERVICES FOR INFANTS AND TODDLERS

In 1986, Congress amended the Education for all Handicapped Children Act (1975) to include a provision for services for infants and toddlers with developmental delays or disabilities and their families. This legislation, previously known as Public Law 99-457, Part H, was renamed the Individuals with Disabilities Education Act (IDEA), Part H in 1990. Eligibility for Part H services is based upon each state's definition of developmental delay. Infants and toddlers who have a medical condition that places them at risk for developmental delay are also eligible for services under Part H.

The original law had three main provisions. Title I established a discretionary program for states to establish a comprehensive system to provide early intervention services to disabled infants from birth until 3 years of age. Title II required states by 1992 to provide a free and appropriate public education and related services to disabled children from age 3. This was a national *mandate* and replaced the earlier law, which *encouraged* states to serve children from age 3. Title III reauthorized programs and services for deaf/blind children and others.

Services for the School-Age Child with ADD

In its Memorandum of September 16, 1991, The United States Department of Education established that students with ADD were covered under Part B of the IDEA. Children with ADD are considered eligible for services under the "other health impaired" category when their ADD is considered a "chronic or acute health problem that results in limited alertness which adversely affects educational performance." This impaired performance must, however, be reflected in the child's schoolwork or behavior and not just be an opinion of the parents. If a child is found eligible for services under IDEA, each school system must provide an appropriate educational program designed to meet the student's unique needs. This is termed an Individualized Educational Program or IEP. The development of an IEP requires the participation of a team of individuals. This team should include the parents, the child (when appropriate), the child's teacher, designated specialists, and a representative of the public agency or institution qualified to provide or supervise special education services for the child.

Under the IDEA, if accommodations are required for the child to function in a particular setting, the institution must either provide the accommodations or justify the refusal to provide them. The Department of Education has addressed the areas of accommodations that appear most appropriate for children with ADD and has provided several examples.* These include the following adaptations in regular education programs:

- Providing a structured learning environment
- Repeating and simplifying instructions and in-class and homework assignments
- Supplementing verbal instructions with visual instructions
- Using behavior management techniques
- Adjusting class schedules

---

*Memorandum, Office of Special Projects and Rehabilitation Services, Department of Education, September 16, 1991, p. 7.

- Modifying test delivery
- Using tape recorders, computer-aided instruction, and audiovisual equipment
- Selecting modified textbooks or workbooks
- Tailoring homework assignments

Other provisions range from consultation of specialists to the child or teacher and other special resources. These may include the following:

- Reducing class size
- Use of one-on-one tutorials
- Classroom aides and note takers
- Involvement of a "services coordinator" to oversee implementation of special programs and services
- Possible modification of nonacademic times such as lunchroom, recess, and physical education.

SERVICES AT THE POSTSECONDARY LEVEL

Accommodations required at the postsecondary level may be covered by the RA (see below) and the ADA. While the institution is under no obligation to change admission standards, course modifications and other accommodations are required by law. Many colleges and universities are seeking to assist the students with ADD by setting up support programs that provide varied accommodations. Adaptations in programming may be available, but the individual must still meet all of the requirements for graduation or admission to a professional school or graduate program.

THE REHABILITATION ACT OF 1973 (RA)

The Rehabilitation Act of 1973 prohibits discrimination against individuals in employment by the federal government and in access to programs conducted by the federal government with federal funds (Section 504). Under the RA, an individual with a disability is defined as one who has a physical or mental impairment that substantially limits a major life activity, has a record of such an impairment, or is regarded as having such an impairment. For children with ADD, this includes learning, and the RA definitely applies to individuals with ADD that substantially limits a major life activity. Postsecondary education is usually covered under this act as most colleges receive federal funds and therefore are subject to the RA.

Section 504, like the IDEA, requires schools receiving federal funds to address the needs of the child with a disability and provide a free and appropriate public education. There is, however, an important difference between the two laws. While IDEA requires that a child have a disability that requires special education services and that, as such, the child be classified as eligible for services, Section 504 qualifies a person on the basis of his having an impairment that limits one of life's major activities, including learning. Thus a child with ADD who does not need special education services under the IDEA may be qualified to receive accommodations under Section 504 of the RA.

A student who thus qualifies under the RA can then have a 504 Accommodation Plan drawn up to serve his or her needs. Most school systems elect to deal with this process at the level of the child's local school. Child study or intervention assistance teams are set up to ascertain the individual students' needs within that environment and to create the 504 Accommodation Plan. This plan assures that all parties involved are aware of the services that a particular student requires. Successful accommodation plans usually undertake to match a solution to a particular need. These solutions are usually easy to implement and relatively inexpensive. They do, however, require flexibility and sometimes creative problem solving approaches. A sample 504 Accommodation Plan follows in Exhibit 2 on pp. 200–201.

The above accommodations are certainly not all-inclusive but serve as examples of the kinds of accommodations that benefit the student with ADD and the ease with which they can be addressed even within the regular education setting.

Several of these examples are appropriate for all students, but others may vary according to the age of the student and the classroom setting. However, in order for accommodations to be successful, they must be applied consistently, and it is here, in many instances that problems frequently arise.

THE AMERICANS WITH DISABILITIES ACT (ADA)

Unlike the previous two laws, the ADA's protections do not depend on the receipt of federal funds. It was designed to prevent discrimination against individuals with disabilities in private sector employment, state and local government employment and programs, and public accommodations. It also covers children with disabilities and requires all educational institutions (public and private) other than those with religious affiliations to provide for the needs of children with ADD.

In Title II of the Act, all public schools are prohibited from the denial of educational services, programs, and activities to students with disabilities once they are enrolled. Nonsectarian private schools are likewise so prohibited and covered under Title III of the Act. The private school does not, however, have to provide special education programs nor does it have to change its admission requirements, but it is required to take whatever steps are reasonable to accommodate qualified disabled applicants.

What specific accommodations are required under the ADA for adults with ADD in the workplace? Reasonable accommodations as defined by Latham & Latham (1990) in their book *Succeeding in the Workplace* (pp. 119–120), are those required to ensure equal opportunity in the application process; those that allow the individual to function on the job; and those that allow the individual to enjoy the same rights and privileges as those without disabilities. Reasonable accommodations for individuals with ADD in the workplace may include the following:

EXHIBIT 2
504 Accommodation Plan

It has been determined_____(Name of Student)

School: _____   Date of Birth: _____

Teacher: _____   Grade: _____

qualifies as a handicapped individual under Section 504 of the Rehabilitation Act of 1973 and the following *areas of need* have been established:

- A. Distractibility
- B. Missing assignments
- C. Poor handwriting
- D. Inability to sit for long periods
- E. Calling out behavior
- F. Poor test performance

Accommodations in accordance with Section 504 guidelines agreed upon
by the school to meet these individual needs are:

A.   1. Preferential seating/near the teacher or away from distracting
          stimuli such as doors and windows.

      2. Cueing the student to remain on task.

      3. Standing near the student to give directions or lightly touch-
          ing the student on the shoulder to refocus.

B.   1. Assigning a homework buddy.

      2. Providing a copy of all assignments in writing.

      3. Providing a weekly or monthly syllabus.

      4. Conducting a weekly assignment completion checkup.

C.   1. Allowing computer-produced or typewritten assignments.

2. Shortening assignments or breaking them down into smaller segments.

3. Giving extra time to complete written assignments

D. 1. Giving frequent breaks.

2. Allowing movement within the classroom.

3. Assigning student tasks that will allow for walking around inside or outside the class.

E. 1. Instituting a behavior-management program.

2. Reward appropriate behavior.

F. 1. Giving untimed tests if necessary.

2. Requiring fewer correct responses to achieve a grade and/or allowing more objective answers rather than long essays.

3. Giving part or all of the test orally.

4. Giving frequent short quizzes and avoiding long exams.

5. Reading test item to the student.

6. Allowing open-book tests.

7. Giving take-home tests or extra credit material.

8. Allowing the student to tape answers on a tape recorder.

Participants present at
development of PLAN: _____

Parent's signature: _____

Child's signature (when appropriate): _____

Case manager: _____   Date: _____

- Part-time or modified work schedules
- Job restructuring or reassignment
- Modifying equipment
- Adjusting or modifying examinations, training, materials or policies
- Providing readers or interpreters
- Making the workplace readily accessible for people with disabilities

CONCLUSION

The individual with ADD may be covered by the laws prohibiting discrimination against persons with disabilities. From infancy through adulthood, individuals with disabilities should be provided with the necessary programs and accommodations that will allow them to function to their full potential.

REFERENCES

CH.ADD. (1993). Educational Rights for Children with ADD. CH.ADD FACTS, #4.

Davila, Robert R. Memorandum from Robert R. Davila, Assistant Secretary to Chief State School Officers, September 16, 1991, United States Department of Education, Office of Special Education and Rehabilitative Services.

Latham, P. S., & Latham, P. H. (1993). *Attention deficit disorder and the law.* Washington, DC: JKL Communications.

Latham, P. S., & Latham, P. H. (1993). *Learning disabilities and the law.* Washington, DC: JKL Communications.

Latham, P. S., & Latham, P. H. (1994). *Succeeding in the workplace.* Washington, DC: JKL Communications.

National Center for Law and Learning Disabilities. (1994). *Higher education services for students with LD and ADD: A legal guide.* Cabin John, MD: Author.

Quinn, P. O. (Ed.). (1994). *ADD and the college student.* New York: Magination Press.

Chapter 10

CONCLUSION

As we have seen in the previous chapters, ADD is a complex disorder that affects individuals throughout their lives. Biochemical deficits and neurologic dysfunction (Chapter 1) are probably present from birth, resulting in the atypical infants described in Chapter 2. Attentional deficits and hyperactivity become manifest in the toddler, with evidence of developmentally inappropriate levels of functioning in attention and motor control (Chapter 3). Definitive diagnosis is made in most cases by elementary school, but this population continues to be heterogeneous, with multiple difficulties across various areas of functioning, including behavior, peer relationships, self-esteem, emotional control, and learning (Chapter 4).

We are now fully aware, as presented in Chapters 5 and 6, that contrary to prior beliefs, the disorder does not resolve itself in adolescence or young adulthood, although some symptoms may be more manageable if diagnosed and treated properly. Adults with ADD provide a whole new frontier for diagnosis, treatment, and further research (Chapter 7) as they continue to present with attention, memory, and organizational deficits.

Despite the continuing and pervasive attention deficits seen at each developmental stage, individuals with ADD present with different needs and difficulties depending on their age and environment. These various issues must be addressed in a comprehensive manner with a complex, multimodal treatment program, as discussed in Chapter 8. Laws are now in place (Chapter 9) that make advocacy for the disabled somewhat easier; however, achieving this total treatment program is not always easy. The practitioner is in a unique position to give guidance and encouragement along the way. In Exhibit 3 on pp. 205–209, I hope to summarize the needs and difficulties encountered at each developmental stage and to reiterate the points that need to be covered in any comprehensive treatment program.

Over the years, I have found that it is ultimately the individuals or families who can access such a complete treatment program that have the best prognosis for a successful outcome. Through programs that address their needs, individuals with ADD become empowered as they try to cope with the many aspects of the disorder.

In order to offer effective treatment, the clinician must realize that the individual with ADD belongs to a group composed of a very heterogeneous population and that all individuals with ADD are not alike. Careful evaluation for comorbid psychiatric conditions is essential and requires special training and experience in this area. In addition, the mental health professional must be aware that most primary care physicians are not trained nor do they have an interest in the area of psychopharmacology pertaining to these disorders. When making referrals for this aspect of the treatment, the professional should be wary and seek out only those individuals with the expertise to handle the polypharmacy sometimes needed to address all aspects of the patient's symptomatology.

EXHIBIT 3
Developmental Stage Outline

ATYPICAL INFANTS AND TODDLERS

Needs:

Self-regulation including:
Arousal
Deviant attentiveness
Crying
Irritability
Sleep disorders
Structure
Limit setting
Control issues
Dependency
Parental–child interactions that are clearly affected

Difficulties:

Neurologic dysfunction
Overaggressive/oppositional behaviors
Short attention span
Hyperactivity
Low threshold of frustration
Temper tantrums
Sleep disorders
Accident proneness

Treatment Program:

Parent education and counseling
Behavior modification
Environmental manipulation
Educational intervention—nursery school/Head Start
Occupational/physical therapy
Play therapy
Medication
Diet

THE PRESCHOOL CHILD WITH ADD

Needs:

Proper nursery school placement
Increasing attention span for learning
Increasing social awareness and interaction

Difficulties:

Hyperactivity
Aggression
Poor socialization
Learning delays
Developmental issues when ADHD is not the only problem

Treatment Program:

Parent and teacher education
Behavior management
Environmental manipulation
Proper diet
Medication
Other therapies as indicated (occupational, physical, language)

THE ELEMENTARY SCHOOL CHILD

This is a critical transition point. The child is no longer just at home but exposed to teachers, coaches, and other parents and children with different levels of understanding and tolerance for ADD symptoms and behaviors.

Needs:

Understanding of the characteristics of the ADD for a particular child (No one has all of them.)

Attention problems
Distractibility
Impulsivity
Hyperactivity
Mood swings/disorders
Irritability
Insatiability
Social skills problems
Sleep disorders
Motor incoordination

Proper diagnosis/treatment
ADHD vs. ADD—a distinction that is often missed
Self-awareness/self-advocacy

Difficulties:

Poor self-esteem

Poor peer relationships
Learning difficulties and underachievement—40 percent also have true
learning disabilities

Treatment Program:

Parent/child/teacher education
Behavioral therapy
Self-esteem enhancement
Biofeedback/cognitive therapies after age nine
Individual psychotherapy
Medication
Educational interventions including a 504 Accommodation Plan
Classroom adaptations
Tutoring
Other related services(occupational, physical, and language
therapies)

The Adolescent/High School Student

Needs:

Not wanting to feel different, as identification with peers and peer cul-
ture increases
Other social issues—dating, driving, etc.
Academic demands increasing
Sports participation increasing
Separation from parents and family
Exert control over impulses and drives need to delay gratification, plan
ahead, and establish long-range goals

Difficulties:

High level of anger and frustration
Poor self-esteem
Mood disorders
Depression in adolescents with ADD, either primary or secondary
Inappropriate social skills
Confusion about goals and future
Lack of perseverance (dropouts)
Need for immediate gratification
Denial
Poor academic achievement (increasing demands, not in as structured
an environment as before)

Stopping medication or other treatments that have worked
previously
Accidents

Treatment Program:

Individual therapy to increase self-awareness and deal with issues and
treatment of depression
Support groups
School accommodations:
504 plan
A fifth year before college
Test accommodations, especially the SATs
Medication:
Combination therapies to affect various neurotransmitters, seroto-
nin, dopamine, and norepinephrine, and address symptoms of
aggressivity, hyperarousal, and anxiety
College placement and career counseling

THE POSTSECONDARY STUDENT

Again a transition point as the student seeks an opportunity to "start
fresh" without the help needed previously; an "I can do this alone" attitude noted.

Needs:

Organizational skills—little support available
Complexity of getting everything done overwhelms, so nothing gets
done
Verbal skills:
Inappropriate word choices or word retrieval problems during oral
presentations or conversations. These are also compromised by
anxiety or attentional problems. Tendency to interrupt or not lis-
ten during conversations.
Academic skills:
Reading problems resulting from difficulty persevering or concentrat-
ing on material
Note taking may be impossible as it uses two processing skills simulta-
neously
Writing skills requiring sustained attention and organizational skills
Impulse control/decision making:
Problem in choosing major/changing major frequently
Frequent number of dropped or incomplete courses

Difficulties:

Spectrum mood disorders/irritability/depression/low frustration
tolerance
Underachievement/poor academic performance
Disorganization/ forgetfulness
Stopping therapies, including medication
Treatment Program:
Therapy
Support groups
Counseling: college and career
Adaptations and modifications
Medication, including combination therapies
Auxiliary aids: calendars, earplugs, laptops, etc.
Metacognitive or self-regulatory skills

ADULTS WITH ADD

Needs:

Organization of time and space
Impulse control/decision making:
Changes jobs frequently
Less job satisfaction
Frequent moves
Marital difficulties

Difficulties:

Disorganization and forgetfulness
Spectrum of mood disorders
Feeling of never having accomplished what one is capable of doing
Procrastination
Anger/low frustration tolerance
Alcoholism and drug abuse

Treatment Program:

Therapy—individual and group
Medication—may need higher doses and combination therapy
Career counseling
Adaptations and modifications on the job
Auxiliary aids

COMORBIDITY AND ATTENTION DEFICIT DISORDER

Biederman and colleagues (1991, 1992, 1993) have presented evidence indicating that the majority of persons with ADD have at least one and sometimes more than one additional psychiatric disorder. These disorders include depression, tics, Tourette's syndrome, behavior disorders, substance abuse, obsessive-compulsive disorder, anxiety disorder, and learning disabilities. Barkley, summarizing a number of studies, indicated that 75% of individuals with ADD show depression into adulthood, 23 to 45% have juvenile convictions, and as many as 27% may abuse alcohol (Barkley, 1990).

While the presence of these comorbid disorders in individuals diagnosed with ADD is not disputed, the clinician must always be cognizant of the characteristics inherent in ADD itself that may mimic these conditions. The cognitive impairments seen in individuals with ADD may indeed lead to academic underachievement, but do they constitute a specific learning disability? Is it possible that the hyperarousal seen in ADD combined with depressed mood may be misdiagnosed as a bipolar disorder? Could poor self-esteem and depressed mood be mistaken for major depression? Or does ADD, in itself, lead to substance abuse? All are valid questions that the clinician treating individuals with ADD must confront and attempt to answer.

COGNITIVE FUNCTIONING IN ADD

In the majority of cases of ADD, an impairment of cognitive functioning affecting areas of attention, inhibition, planning, and sequencing can also be seen. These cognitive inefficiencies have collectively been referred to as the executive function disorders by Denckla (1989) and Pennington (1991). That the learning disabilities seen in association with ADD are due to these primary deficiencies in planning, organization, and motivation has also been postulated (Joseph, 1987). While children with ADD may be diagnosed with specific learning disabilities, these are probably not due to this primary cognitive deficit (McGee & Share, 1988).

Douglas (1980) has looked at this concept of impaired cognitive functioning and compared children with ADHD and LD. Results suggest that there may be different types of cognitive disabilities underlying the two disorders. More specifically, studies indicated that the children with ADHD have particular difficulty with the strategies of problem-solving skills. Children with ADHD also tended to do less well on tasks that required memory in a free recall situation.

The inefficient cognitive strategies displayed by young hyperactive children have also been found to persist into adulthood. In a study conducted by Hopkins and coworkers (1979), adults with ADD were seen to be at a distinct disadvantage in choosing an alternative in situations when the response is uncertain and when they must select the relevant stimuli from a complex presentation. They also were more easily distractible by irrelevant stimuli than controls and less able to inhibit incorrect verbalizations.

This primary cognitive deficit is further postulated to be the underlying cause of both academic underachievement and social deficits. Lambert & Sandoval (1980) reported underachievement in reading or math in 53% of the boys with hyperactivity compared to 11% of the controls in their follow-up study. Similar findings had been reported earlier by Cantwell and Satterfield (1978) with greater than one third of boys with ADHD also having academic performance problems in two of the academic subjects tested.

Successful treatment of ADHD must therefore take cognitive deficits into account. Continuing impairment of cognitive functioning, indeed, may be the factor responsible for the continued underachievement and poor peer relationships seen in individuals despite reduction of the major symptoms of ADD after successful pharmacologic interventions.

BEHAVIORAL DISORDERS

Aggressive and antisocial behaviors are some of the most significant problems associated with ADD. Between 30 and 90% of children with ADD also exhibit significant conduct problems (Hinshaw, 1987). Conduct and oppositional disorders were found in a study of clinically referred children with ADD conducted by Biederman and colleagues (1987b). Likewise, an 8-year prospective follow-up study conducted by Barkley and associates (1990) found that, using DSM-III-R criteria, 59% of the children with hyperactivity were found to have Oppositional Defiant Disorder (ODD) and 43% had a Conduct Disorder. When two standard deviations above the normal mean were used, 60% of adolescents with ADD also showed conduct disorders.

This group remains the most difficult to treat and has the worst prognosis in all follow-up studies, but are these separate disorders or part of ADD itself? In one study, Loeber and associates found that the development of a conduct disorder in boys 8 to 17 was significantly predicted by ADHD (Loeber et al., 1995). However, the work of Loney, suggests that aggression seen in individuals with ADHD is a separate entity and stems from a different source than the attentional deficits (Loney et al., 1978; Milich & Loney, 1979).

SUBSTANCE ABUSE DISORDERS

While ADD alone may not be a factor in increased risk for substance abuse in adolescents and young adults (Weiss & Hechtman, 1993, Feldman et al., 1979), the cooccurrence of these disorders is more common than expected with 23% being the mean rate of ADHD found in the subjects of eight studies of adolescents and adults with substance use disorders. Studies also indicate that between 17 and 45% of adults with

ADHD manifested alcohol abuse or dependence, and between 9 and 30 % manifest drug abuse or dependence (Wilens et al., 1994). Tzelepis and coworkers (1995) also report substance abuse to be a significant problem in adults diagnosed with ADHD with as many as 23% dependent on alcohol, 9% on marijuana, 6% cocaine, and 5% with polydrug dependence.

While the literature demonstrates an association between ADD and substance abuse, it should be clearly stated that children with ADD alone are at a negligible risk for substance abuse. Children whose ADD persists as they get older may be at risk for substance abuse as adolescents and adults (Wilens & Lineham, 1995). Research further indicates that the presence of Conduct Disorder may be a more significant factor than ADD. As many as 20 to 40% of individuals with the dual diagnosis of ADD and conduct disorder may have problems with substance abuse. In all of these cases it appears that the conduct disorder preceded the development of substance abuse (Halikas et al., 1990; Manuzza et al., 1993).

ADD does not cause substance abuse per se, but there may be several factors associated with the disorder that predispose individuals diagnosed with ADD to this condition (Tarter, 1988). These include poor self-esteem, increased incidence of a family history of alcohol abuse (Cantwell, 1972), and symptoms of ADD itself, such as poor impulse control and judgment.

Treatment of this group with ADD and substance abuse requires that both disorders be addressed simultaneously with an initial focus on the individual's substance abuse. Treatment for the ADD should also be provided and should include therapeutic interventions as well as medication to reduce the symptoms of ADHD (Wilens et al., 1994).

TOURETTE'S SYNDROME

Tourette's syndrome (TS) is a complex neuropsychiatric disorder associated with ADD, OCD, learning problems, depression, and motor tics. The incidence of ADD in TS is dramatically higher than found in the general population. More than 50% of children with TS show ADD symptoms. In one study by Comings and Comings (1984), the incidence of ADD was also found to be related to the severity of the Tourette's symptomatology. The frequency of hyperactivity increased with the severity of Tourette's syndrome with hyperactivity present in 32% of the mildly involved, 51% in the moderately involved, and 69% of the severely involved patients. Sex differences were noted, with these figures being significantly higher for males (74%) than for females with the severe form of the disorder.

MOOD DISORDERS

Although mood disorders appear later and may be superimposed on the ADD, comorbidity of depression and ADD has been suggested to be as high as 25% (Biederman, 1987a). This group may represent a more psychiatrically impaired group, with poor long-term prognosis (Gittleman, 1985). There is a higher incidence of mood disorders in parents and close relatives of children and adults with both ADD and a mood disorder than in those with ADD alone (Stewart & Morrison, 1973). Jensen and colleagues (1988) also found an increase in affective symptoms, dysphoria, and dysthymia in children with ADD. These children, however, did not have symptoms of a concurrent conduct disorder. Children who were found to have both a conduct disorder and ADD were more likely to have had a major depressive disorder diagnosed.

Treatment with antidepressants alone or in combination with stimulants is indicated for this select population. A tricyclic antidepressant as a single agent has been particularly effective in treating the symptoms of both depression and/or anxiety and ADD (Donnelly et al., 1986).

ANXIETY DISORDERS

Although these are among the least common conditions reported in children with ADD, Biederman and coworkers (1991) report a comorbid association of anxiety disorders of almost 25% in children with ADD. Children with ADD without hyperactivity may have even higher rates than those with ADHD, as reported by Lahey and colleagues (1987). But do some of these children simply represent a state of hyperarousal and hypervigilance which results in overanxiety or do they represent a true anxiety disorder? The clinician will need to answer this question on a case by case basis.

DIAGNOSIS AND OUTCOME

In general, there is no question that comorbidity enormously complicates the diagnosis and worsens the prognosis, particularly when ADD is associated with a conduct or antisocial personality disorder. Perhaps only as few as 30% of individuals with ADD have this as the sole diagnosis. However, comorbidity can also be the basis for further delineation of these heterogenous populations and thus may assist in designing specific treatment protocols and psychopharmacologic regimens. Outcome, however, remains dependent on clear and precise diagnosis, which addresses both specific symptomatology and other important coexisting variables that will dictate intervention strategies from infancy to adulthood.

REFERENCES

Barkley, R. A. (1990). *Attention deficit hyperactivity disorder: A handbook for diagnosis and treatment.* New York: Guilford Press.

Barkley, R. A., Fischer, M., Edelbrock, E. S., & Smallish, L. (1990). The adolescent outcome of hyperactive children diagnosed by research criteria, I: An eight year prospective follow-up study. *Journal of the American Academy of Child and Adolescent Psychiatry, 9*, 546–557.

Biederman, J., Faraone, S. V., & Lapey, K. (1992). Comorbidity of diagnosis in attention-deficit hyperactivity disorder. In G. Weiss (Ed.), *Attention-deficit hyperactivity disorder, child & adolescent psychiatric clinics of North America.* Philadelphia: Sanders.

Biederman, J., Faraone, S., Spencer, T., & Wilens, T. (1993). Patterns of psychiatric comorbidity, cognition, and psychosocial functioning in adults with ADHD. *American Journal of Psychiatry, 150*, 1792–1798.

Biederman, J., Munir, K., & Knee, D. (1987a). High rate of affective disorders in probands with attention deficit disorder and in their relatives: A controlled family study. *American Journal of Psychiatry, 144*, 330.

Biederman, J., Munir, K., & Knee, D. (1987b). Conduct and oppositional disorder in clinically referred children with attention deficit disorder: A controlled family study. *Journal of the American Academy of Child and Adolescent Psychiatry, 148*, 564.

Biederman, J., Newcomb, J., & Sprich, S. (1991). Comorbidity of ADHD with conduct, depressive, anxiety and other disorders. *American Journal of Psychiatry, 148*, 564–577.

Cantwell, D. P. (1972). Psychiatric illness in families of hyperactive children. *Archives of General Psychiatry, 27*, 414–417.

Cantwell, D. P., & Satterfield, J. H. (1978). Prevalence of academic achievement in hyperactive children. *Journal of Pediatric Psychology, 3*, 168–171.

Comings, D. E., & Comings, B. G. (1984). Tourette's syndrome and attention deficit disorder with hyperactivity: Are they related? *Journal of the American Medical Association, 23*, 138–146.

Denckla, M. B. (1989). Executive function, the overlap zone between attention deficit hyperactivity disorder and learning disabilities. *International Pediatrics, 4*, 155–160.

Donnelly, M., Zametkin, A. J., & Rapoport, J. L. (1986). Treatment of childhood hyperactivity with desipramine: Plasma drug concentration, cardiovascular effects, plasma and urinary catecholamine levels, and clinical response. *Clinical Pharmacology and Therapeutics, 39,* 72–81.

Douglas, V. I. (1980). Self-control techniques, Higher mental process in hyperactive children: Implications for training. In R. M. Knights & D. J. Bakker (Eds.), *Treatment of hyperactive and learning disordered children—Current research.* Baltimore, MD: University Park Press.

Feldman, S. A., Denhoff, E., & Denhoff, J. I. (1979). The attention disorders and related syndromes: Outcome in adolescence and young adult life. In L. Stern & E. Denhoff (Eds.), *Minimal brain dysfunction: A developmental approach.* New York: Masson.

Gittleman, R., Mannuzza, S., & Shenker, R. (1985). Hyperactive boys almost grown up. *Archives of General Psychiatry, 42,* 937.

Halikas, J. A., Meller, J., Morce, C., & Lyttle, M. D. (1990). Predicting substance abuse in juvenile offenders: Attention deficit disorder versus aggressivity. *Child Psychology and Human Development, 21,* 49–55.

Hinshaw, S. P. (1987). On the distinction between attention deficits/hyperactivity and conduct problems/aggression in child psychopathology. *Psychological Bulletin, 101,* 443–463.

Hopkins, J., Perlman, T., Hechtman, L., & Weiss, G. (1979). Cognitive style in adults originally diagnosed as hyperactives. *Journal of Child Psychology and Psychiatry, 20,* 209–216.

Joseph, J. (1987). Learning disabilities due to primary deficiency of planning, organization, and motivation. *Neurology, 37* (supp), 221.

Lahey, B. B., Schaughency, E. A., Hynd, G. W., et al. (1987). Attention deficit disorder with and without hyperactivity: Comparison of behavioral characteristics of clinic-referred children. *Journal of the American Academy of Child and Adolescent Psychiatry, 26,* 718–723.

Lambert, N. M., & Sandovalo, J. (1980). The prevalence of learning disabilities in a sample of children considered hyperactive. *Journal of Abnormal Child Psychology, 8,* 33–50.

Loeber, R., Green, S. M., Keenan, K., & Lahey, B. B. (1995). Which boys will fare worse?: Early predictors of the onset of conduct disorder in a six-year longitudinal study. *Journal of the American Academy of Child and Adolescent Psychiatry, 34,* 499–509.

Manuzza, S., Klein, R. G., Bessler, A., et al. (1993). Adult outcomes of hyperactive boys. *Archives of General Psychiatry, 50,* 565–576.

McGee, R., & Share, D. L. (1988). Attention deficit-hyperactivity and academic failure: Which comes first and what should be treated? *Journal of the American Academy of Child and Adolescent Psychiatry, 27,* 318–325.

Pennington, B. F. (1991). *Diagnosing learning disorders: A neuropsychological framework.* New York: Guilford Press.

Stewart, M. A., & Morrison, J. R. (1973). Affective disorder among the relatives of hyperactive children. *Journal of Child Psychology and Psychiatry, 14,* 209–212.

Tarter, R. E. (1988). Are there inherited behavioral traits that predispose to substance abuse? *Journal of Consulting and Clinical Psychology, 56,* 189–196.

Tzelepis, A., Schubiner, H., & Warbasse, L. H. (1995). Differential diagnosis and psychiatric co-morbidity patterns in adult attention deficit disorder. In K. G. Nadeau (Ed.), *A comprehensive guide to attention deficit disorder in adults.* New York: Brunner/ Mazel.

Weiss, G., & Hechtman, L. T. (1993). *Hyperactive children grown up.* (2nd ed.). New York: Guilford Press.

Wilens, T. E., Biederman, J., Spencer, T. J., & Frances, R. J. (1994). Comorbidity of attention deficit hyperactivity disorder and the psychoactive substance use disorders. *Hospital and Community Psychiatry, 45,* 421–435.

Wilens, T. E., & Lineham, C. E. (1995). ADD and substance abuse: An intoxicating combination. *Attention!, 3,* 24–31.

NAME INDEX

SUBJECT INDEX